Young Children's Talent
& It's Method

by Dr. SHINICHI SUZUKI

Translated by KYOKO SELDEN

© 1996, 1949 Dr. Shinichi Suzuki
Sole Publisher for the world except Japan:
Summy-Birchard Inc.
exclusively distributed by
Warner Bros. Publications
15800 NW 48th Avenue
Miami, FL 33014
All rights reserved   Printed in USA

ISBN: 0-87487-770-9
1 3 5 7 9 8 6 4 2

YOUNG CHILDREN'S TALENT EDUCATION AND ITS METHOD
by Shinichi Suzuki
translated by Kyoko Selden

National Association of Young Children's Education
1946

Reprinted in the original Japanese in 1979 to commemorate the 25th National Concert.
Corresponds to the edited version in the *Complete Works,* Vol. 1, pp. 65-179.

Table of Contents

PREFACE

After the Meiji Restoration of 1868, our country's education seemed to have demonstrated remarkable development, and the Japanese people felt confident that their nation was outstanding. However, this was a subjective view created through pride. If we calmly evaluate the ability demonstrated by the Japanese people to this day, we must say that in face we have failed to demonstrate sufficient ability to keep pace with the cultures of advanced countries of the world.

What is causing us to be a nation with such a low level of ability? We need to discover the real root of the problem.

A nation's rise or fall depends upon its people's ability, and this is the source of culture. The question of a nation's ability is, in brief, the question of education. Then, what flaws do we have in education? In focusing on this question, I would like to point out that we have been making two great errors in education since the Meiji era.

The first is the single-track elementary school system, whether the *shogakko* established following the Meiji Restoration or the present *kokumin gakko*.[1] We have been strictly abiding by the compulsory education which forces every child without exception to start with the alphabet and arithmetic at age six, that is, a *homogeneous mass education system.* This homogenizes the development of our talents, and at the same time hampers in the extreme the development of the nation's outstanding ability. I view this as the first flaw in our approach to education.

The second is our careless enforcement of methods that blight the Japanese people's talent without any research into methods for developing human talent.

Through more than a dozen years of instructing little children aged three and four, I have come to know clearly what superior ability children can demonstrate before age seven. It is not surprising, I realized, that long ago Arai Hakuseki (1657-1725), a Confucian scholar and politician in the mid-Edo period, lectured on the Four Books and Five Classics, classical Confucian writings, by the age of seven. This ability should not be viewed as a unique ability of that single child; if instructed skillfully, many ordinary children I know can manifest ability which almost equals it. Heaven's logic is clear. A sapling left alone

---

1. The name changed back to *shogakko* in 1947, the year after this book was written.

for a long time without effort being put into its nurturing looks thin and poor; however hard you may subsequently work on this plant, however much fertilizer you may give it, it will not yield beautiful large flowers worthy of display in an exhibit. Everyone knows what careful attention growers pay to raising their plants and how much they study the method of raising them without contradicting heaven's logic, in order to produce great flowers. How can a person indifferent to nurturing plans produce superior flowers? Yet how is it with our education system? No effort is directed to the most crucial fostering, that of young children's talent; rather, it is encouraged that neither the alphabet nor arithmetic be taught at home so that children throughout the country enter school in the perfect white paper or tabula rasa state. We adopt the system which forces the entire nation to start over again at age seven with the alphabet and their one, two, threes.

The result of abiding by this flawed educational system for the long period since the Meiji Restoration is, namely, today's Japan. Before we knew it, in terms of ability we dropped behind in the world's cultural progress. To save this falling nation and construct a path to let it rouse itself for tomorrow's prosperity, I believe, is the first project we should immediately undertake. Until this blocked path is opened up, we will trace the fate of sad decline by the months and years.

Kiso Fukushima,
May 1946

A NATION'S PROSPERITY DEPENDS UPON WOMEN'S STRENGTH

Who is able to look without tears at present-day Japan as it is and its people as they are? When will we be able to see again a beautiful world where we yield to one another, help one another, and live with warm hearts, hand in hand? At present, our desolate hearts are occupied with assertion of rights, selfish obsession, and self-interest. While the bitterness of such hearts swirls around the entire country, the ignorant nation is tracing the path of degradation. Can our base, miserable present plight represent after all the true nature of the Japanese people? Is the essence of three thousand years of tradition and Japanese culture built over long years no more, after all, than this?

Looking back now, I realize regretfully that the laborious efforts by administrators and educators since the early Meiji years were unable to produce fine flowers or bear fruit. Had Japan's education in the past been vigorous and full of life, and had we become a truly cultured, outstanding nation, we would not have erred so badly as to let our nation fall to today's misfortune. Even if we had been defeated in the war, we would have saved ourselves from such a miserable social situation. Sadly, Japan today is nothing but an uneducated nation. However, since grieving does not help, we of today must seek a proper path for tomorrow's Japan. Japan has not been reduced to today's sad situation for no discernible reason; the cause of the decline definitely can be found in Japan's past.

Food problems are grave for today's Japan, but a more fundamental problem exists in education, which is the key to the survival of the nation. In other words, only there is there light, and only there a path toward tomorrow's destiny. I believe, moreover, that the greatest power toward opening up the path exists in women, especially mothers.

If young children's ability comes to be fostered with great care by mothers nationwide, perhaps in ten years the foundation will be created for Japan to become a nation which can demonstrate exceptional ability. If, moreover, innovations are made in Japan's education system during the interval, I am certain that Japan will, in the following decade, begin to demonstrate its power to the world as an outstanding nation.

In short, two decades will suffice to make Japan the world's leading nation, and if the entire country concentrates on this vital point, I do not hesitate to say with confidence that our culture will last long. For this, I feel the need to encourage Japanese women to rise with great force. Without women's power, this great enterprise for the nation's cultural flourishing could hardly be achieved.

I make a plea to all Japanese mothers to start early education in order to make your children Japanese who can demonstrate fine ability. Be it the alphabet, math, music, art, or anything else. Select just one category, and, focusing on in, start teaching your children little by little every day, never rushing and never resting, with good understanding of each of the conditions for developing ability which I will now describe. Perhaps at first there will be much disappointment, for children will not demonstrate such ability as you desire. Then remember the earliest period when you taught your babies to speak. No matter how slender the ability is at first, do not be disappointed at all but know that this is the sprouting period for children and make efforts to repeat the same thing, without resting, despairing, or rushing. It is the same thing with planting vegetable seeds. They do not sprout immediately; however, they will some day. Not only that - once they sprout, they grow even while you watch them.

Continue the same effort with your children, for half a year at first. What strength will they show? I feel I can already imagine your joy and surprise after that interval. To a large extent, children grow depending upon how they are raised.

If children are trained with concentration in a single area for two or three years, their ability will startle their parents and others around them. This training should be continued until they are seven. In some cases, it is effective to invite an outstanding instructor to guide the child. Even in that case, it is crucial that the child grow with the mother's help; do not forget that the instructor is no more than a guide who can show the best path. For only by the mother's love and patience does children's ability develop most richly.

By the time they are seven, some children will demonstrate ability beyond the graduation level of present-day elementary school. If so, voices will naturally arise saying that those outstanding children should somehow continue to be guided higher. When these voices become loud, innovation in Japan's educational system will for the first time be urgently required; schools will have to be founded immediately for properly educating such children.

Isn't it foolish to leave children uneducated from such misgivings as that, even if children develop ability through early education, they will have to start from the alphabet again at elementary school, which makes the past efforts meaningless? Please think about this so that you will not spoil your children's precious learning period entirely through this futile anticipation. Even if no educational innovation is carried out and your children have to enter elementary school, it will be fine, to move ahead vigorously, independently of school, with the one thing each has pursued from early childhood. Since children who have developed ability to that extent will handle other school subjects well without special efforts and achieve fine records, you will have no particular worry. This has been the case with my students: while demonstrating the ability to play concert repertoire on the violin, they achieve excellent records at elementary school. If we first help them develop outstanding ability in one area, we ought to know that children can use that ability to absorb other things easily. In the worst case, there will be no educational innovation; in order to assure great innovation in Japan's educational system as soon as possible, we must vigorously stir public opinion, while also starting political movements.

Fortunately, women have aquired the vote, and a few representatives have been elected to the Diet. This will allow political movements to advance in women's hands. However, even more effective than that would be for mothers throughout the country to start today their children's talent and character education. This would certainly result in more achievements than anything else and would, in turn, help solidify public opinion. No other women's movement could be as powerful and meaningful as this. Start early education for your child as soon as possible, thus putting into practice en masse the nation's great enterprise. Japanese women's awareness of this mission will, I believe, be the very first step toward the nation's most powerful development.

The above is my serious prayer for women throughout Japan. As long as mothers hold the key to the nation's rise or fall, women's awareness of their mission is Japan's awareness. "Like mother, like child" is a truth. If you look at the child, you can tell how great the mother is. A learned mother does not necessarily raise a fine child; only those who are great as human beings raise outstanding children. Bearing this truth in mind will clarify the direction to be emphasized in Japan's child education.

A FLAWED EDUCATIONAL SYSTEM AND NEW UNDERSTANDING

"Children's ability, left alone, asserts itself from within through an inner need as they grow" - this seems to be the lazy thought of most people. Despite this expectation, no matter how many years parents wait, no special power springs out of their children to surprise or please them. "So after all, my child has only normal ability," they think, and gradually give up.

People commonly value rarities more than is desirable, and this applies to humans: when rumor has it that this child is uncommon and that child is a genius, people regard them as totally special presences, elevating them to a great height as if they were mysteries beyond others' reach. However, this is a careless misunderstanding; the ability demonstrated by children receiving attention as being prodigies or geniuses may in fact be the kind which may naturally be expected from human beings and which many ordinary children, including your own, may be able to attain if given the chance. Further, I wonder if people may be ignorant of the fact that the kind of ability they think is common in society is in reality the *lowest level of ability* humans can display, close to inability with no demonstration of talent. Neither scholars nor citizens discuss this; they do not even think about it.

In other words, we may be making a great mistake in regarding as average many children who demonstrate the lowest level of ability, simply because no study has been made on the amount of ability human beings can naturally develop. Since even scholars preach about "inborn talent" and "an extraordinary presence," people tend to believe it blindly. Therefore, they think the important issue of children's ability development is a matter of innate destiny beyond human control, and don't concern themselves with it, leaving all questions of child ability to the gods.

It is indeed sad that parents think this way. Ideally, parents should think seriously about how it is possible to develop their children's ability and help them grow as human beings with active brains. That they give up, thinking they can do nothing about what is inborn, is due to a lack of knowledge about the nature of children, which is really unfortunate for the children. This can be compared to the unhappy situation of seedlings that are left without even water.

The parents of children reputed to be geniuses or prodigies, no matter how they refuse to acknowledge their involvement, were always interested in the small strengths the children showed when stimulated by their first motivations, and fostered their ability through considerable daily effort. In other words, in this connection there should be no error whatsoever about heaven's logic that where there is an effect there is a cause.

When one of my young students, Koji Toyota, performed Dvořák's "Humoresque" at the Japan Youth Hall at two years and five or six months, the *Asahi* wrote about him in the following day's paper as if he were a genius. However, I know that this boy did not suddenly demonstrate that ability. Koji's father, also my student, played the violin every day. Growing in such an environment, Koji was given a small violin by his father and received daily instruction from him; thus he was able to play the piece. The result, which caused some to see genius in him, stemmed in fact from his father's effort to develop the child's ability.

We ought to have enough understanding to think it natural that, with a parent's fine effort, a child can demonstrate this kind of ability as early as two years and five or six months. As stated earlier, I firmly believe that heaven's logic of cause and effect never betrays us. Therefore, even among those who are said to have demonstrated true genius, I am convinced that we find no example in which outstanding ability developed without either the stimulation toward ability called "environment," which is its cause, or the important element called "effort," which develops it.

Those who write the biographies of true geniuses can record the facts only after they have fully learned about their daily living environment in early childhood, and, sometimes in addition to this, the environment of their era, the method of ability development their parents used, and so on. Biographies written by those who do not research all the important causal facts cannot record the truth because they tend to describe their hero as a character endowed with mysterious power from birth. If superior biographers could always convey the facts in precise detail as to what caused geniuses and great men to develop their superior ability, people of later ages would greatly benefit. However, in most biographies the examination of causes is insufficient, and only the report on results startles people.

In brief, we need to think seriously about our children of today and the future, without becoming misled or fettered by such superficial words as genius and prodigy. If all Japanese people gain sufficient knowledge of the ability development of their own children, and begin talent education of small children by the proper method, Japan will soon be able to demonstrate its ability to the world as an outstanding nation. I am expressing my belief in this book with a wish to realize such an era as soon as possible. Out of this desire, I have made it my job for more than a dozen years already, to study the development of children's ability. Through this study, I have discovered that *every child who can speak normally has the potential to develop outstanding ability.* This was a big discovery even to myself. Since then I have been teaching many children in order to prove this fact.

In fact every child has the potential to develop amazing ability. The reason that children in the past have grown without doing so is, in brief, that their parents made no efforts to induce and foster their outstanding ability. The bud of ability dries out, the seedling of talent which should demonstrate outstanding ability becomes so thin and slender that it is irrecoverable. Even if one makes painstaking efforts to grow that thin seedling, it is too late. We must ponder the fact that timing plays an important role in human as well as plant growth.

If we wish to make Japan a leading nation in the world, regardless of the fields we have in mind, we must first know heaven's logic as shown in the greatness of nature, and pay attention to the laws of nature.

In order to let beautiful, large chrysanthemums bloom, master growers first make careful efforts to nurture the seedlings. They never cease to study because they need to know heaven's logic and wisely adjust to nature's demands. Through their efforts, the growers know when the seedlings grow beautifully whether these seedlings will have large, superior blossoms. Even they can do nothing about seedlings which have started to wither.

Heaven reveals natural logic clearly in front of us. In this revelation we ought to find a big lesson: seedlings wither when no efforts are made and the necessary nurturing does not follow. Again, even a master grower cannot raise such seedlings so that they have superior, large blossoms which would win prizes at an exhibit. This is yet another hint heaven has given us.

I think we must reflect deeply on these hints shown by heaven. As though to portray the contrast between heavenly logic and the present-day education in Japan, the Ministry of Education to this day has carried out uniform education under the single elementary school system, and officials of the Ministry have even indicated in radio lectures that as long as uniform education is given in elementary school they would like parents to refrain from teaching their children the alphabet and arithmetic before school and to send them to school in the perfect white paper condition. In other words, the Ministry wants all Japanese children to be left alone and taught nothing for the six seedling years, and insists on this system. Whenever I hear this kind of broadcast, I feel truly miserable. This lack of understanding of human ability accelerates the decline in the Japanese people's ability. At this rate, the prosperity of the nation is hard to envision, and I am sad thinking of how long it might be until the Japanese wake from this nightmare.

In retrospect, the greatest cause of Japan's miserable fate today is *the education system newly established in the early years of Meiji, that is, the elementary school system aimed at unified education.* No one realized that the great educational innovation of the mass education method itself, intended to educate Japanese people all at once so as to eliminate illiteracy, ended in creating great obstacles to the entire nation's ability to advance. The appearance of superior individuals has been hampered by this, and the potential of the Japanese people is still forced to wither at the seedling stage.

I would like to say with confidence: Japanese will never be able to produce outstanding individuals as long as they conform to such a uniform elementary school system.

Long ago Arai Hakuseki, at the age of only seven, is said to have lectured on the major Chinese Confucian documents called the Four Books and the Five Classics. I am sure there are many other examples of such achievement. As is well known, the government-run Confucian Academy at Yushima had a system of regularly administering fairly difficult academic examinations to young samurai children. Provincial governments likewise adopted an educational system similar to these state exams. On looking back, we see that this system was much more powerful than today's uniform elementary school system. At least paths were prepared for producing outstanding individuals. However, even if parents today give early education to their children, raising them like Arai Hakuseki, these children must retrace their steps from the level of the Four Books and Five Classics to the alphabet and receive uniform education. So it is natural that no one now seriously tries to foster children's ability from an early age. Through this sabotage of family education over a long period of time since the Meiji era, we should realize how much the Japanese have clipped and destroyed their own good qualities, degrading themselves into mediocrity.

Let me ask those of you who think of heaven's logic and are persuaded by what I write here to choose *just one area* for your children, whether reading or music, and start *early education.* I will explain the method of instruction in later chapters.

At age three or four, children are already ripe enough to start receiving instruction. I would like you to see in actuality what kind of strength can grow when you train them daily until age seven. The amazing ability they naturally develop is already familiar to me through my personal instruction of children between the ages of three and six or seven for over a dozen years. It is wrong to judge the ability of children we will raise by the ability of children we have known. Instructed skillfully, every child can develop an extremely high level of ability, which is pleasing to parents, although at the same time it is no good if parents feel proud thinking their children may be prodigies.

Some worry that if children use their brains too much in their early years, they may become feeble or damage their brains from overwork. However, no such outcome was seen during my experience; it is nothing more than conjecture. I would like to detail my idea on this problem in a later chapter.

Now, what better person is there to instruct children than the mother? The mother's love, her patience, and her dreams make the strength of instruction more powerful than anything else. Even when the child has an outstanding teacher, the one who puts the training into practice is the mother. It is of course wonderful if the father lends his strength to the young child's ability development. However, since in many cases the family situation does not allow him to, it is acceptable that he is just a good cooperator. Usually the mother bears the heavy responsibility of nurturing the child in every area, including health, ability, and character. This can only be heavenly providence.

In any case, I would like to dedicate this book to all who have children, and to explain what ability is and how to foster ability and character.

Under the title "Special Elementary School Education," I once wrote about the importance of ability development for young children; the urgent need for founding special high-level elementary schools which require an entrance examination; and the reason that the current system, which allows *no alternatives to elementary school,* would certainly result in the nation's decline. However, since this was wartime, such writing was not deemed to please the authorities, and it was withheld from publication.

This is an issue that has much to do with the rise or fall of the nation, and I believe that there is much cause for worry about the future of our people if we follow present trends. Despite the fact that I am no education specialist, I write down my beliefs here, eagerly wishing that more and more people will understand this problem and that our country's education system will improve as soon as possible.

ABILITY DEMONSTRATED IN LANGUAGE

What made me aware of ordinary children's quite outstanding ability and motivated me to undertake the study of this ability was focusing my eyes on the following question: Why is it that *every child has the ability to learn smoothly and beautifully this difficult thing called spoken language,* which has such a complex structure?

Languages, and Japanese in particular, have extremely large vocabularies, and syntaxes that are complex and diversified. Yet everywhere in Japan children demonstrate the ability to use their difficult language with absolute freedom.

What causes children to develop such outstanding ability? This question led to the following others which suggested themselves to me as research projects: Can it be that there is in speech a principle of the best instruction for ability development, and that it fosters children's ability smoothly because its method is right? and Can it be that children have a basic quality, that is, talent, ability, or brain power, which they can develop beautifully if instructed properly?

In order to solve these interesting and important questions, I first started to study what teaching method is being applied in speech. With this purpose, on observing how infants and small children are daily taught in speech, I realized that every adult was carrying out truly outstanding teaching principles. I thought we ought to recognize, as the world's best teaching method, this instructional approach which fosters one human ability with ease, and try to model every new teaching method or principle after it.

What I will describe in the chapter called "How to Foster Ability" is the result of this study. Depending upon the quality of instruction, it is possible to foster and activate successfully the ability or basic quality, which every child naturally possesses. This is a great, joyful discovery; at the same time the responsibility of those engaged in education must be said to have become greater and clearer.

Based on my study of various instructional conditions in speech, my teaching method follows the same approach adults use in teaching babies how to speak. The result of this instruction was the demonstration by children of ability beyond anything we had ever imagined. More than a dozen years have passed since I started to study this question and teach children. The level of ability of the children I have taught during this interval has certainly surpassed world standards.

How many millions of children are there in the world who cannot cope with math and language, that is, children who have poor records at school? In society at large, they are believed to achieve poorly at school because their brains are poor. Shown their report cards, parents think their children don't have such good brains; teachers also think that way.

Then why is it that those children successfully learn spoken Japanese and demonstrate their ability in that area with absolute freedom?

I find great inconsistency in the commonsense assertion that children who do poorly in math and language have inferior brains. The cause of this flawed judgment is that people have never paid attention to or tried to examine children's ability or potential. Moreover, teachers have lacked crucial self-reflection about the fact that it was because the teaching method was poor that the children achieved poorly. They have evaded their responsibility by ascribing it to children's insufficient ability. It would be reasonable if they limited their criticism to children's lack of diligence or efforts, but it is a great error to blame it on their weak brains as a result of an absence of clear understanding of children's ability.

In order to solve these problems and find clear answers, I thought I must prove that every child who can talk has fine ability. So, accepting invitations to teach privately, I started to teach violin, in which I specialized, to three- and four-year olds. The condition for my taking them as disciples was, of course, no such thing as musical trait; I asked if the child could talk, and took everyone who could. Through the daily habit of practice made possible by the efforts of the parents who followed by words, every one of them has developed ability which amazes adults.

Now that I have been able to prove this by actually trying it, children should be expected to develop the superior level of ability that they do in speech no matter who applies the same method of ability development, as long as it is done with good understanding. When the recognition that every child is capable becomes common sense among ordinary people, this will spontaneously produce outstanding instructors and outstanding approaches. Therefore what is important first is that ordinary people reach proper recognition of children's ability.

In order to seek such recognition, I would like for the sake of reference to indicate here what kind of music my young students were able to play. According to common sense in the past in our country, the violin is such a difficult instrument that even grownups cannot prepare a piece to play in front of people after a year or so of training. However, children under my instruction play a Seitz concerto after one year.

The program below is from the fourth student recital held at Hibiya Public Hall, Tokyo, October 24, 1942, which gathered a full-house audience of 3,500 or 3,600 people. The program indicated the years of training and the children's ages.

❧Program❧

1. **Unison** ....Twinkle Variations
   (4 to 9 months of training)

   Kazuko Yamada, 4;   Keiko Yoshida, 7;
   Yoshiharu Ihara, 4;   Atusko Kusamina, 7;
   Kiyomitsu Takei, 4;   Katsuko Azuma, 7;
   Yuhki Kawada, 6;   Kaoru Umehara, 7;
   Mitsuyo Iisaka, 6;   Akiyuki Hisahara, 6.
   Tomoko Okamoto, 5;

2. **Waltz** ....Reading
   Kyoko Sato (age 5), *10 months of training*

3. **Minuet** ....Beethoven
   Makoto Takamiya (age 6), *10 months of training*

4. **Minuet** ....Boccherini
   Sueko Okochi (age 7), *11 months of training*

5. **Humoresque** ....Dvořák
   Akio Yasuda (age 9), *11 months of training*

6. **Concerto No. 2** ....Seitz
   Ohko Okumura (age 11), *10 months of training*

7. **Gavotte** ....Gossec
   Performed by the above members

8. **Concerto for Two Violins** Bach
   First violin: Koji Toyota, Takeshi Kobayashi
   Second violin: Yoko Ishikawa, Kenji Kobayashi

9. **Concerto No. 2** ....Seitz
   Yoshitaka Torio (age 10), *12 months of training*

10. **Concerto No. 5** ....Seitz
    Teiichi Tanaka (age 7), *12 months of training*

11. **Concerto No. 5** ....Seitz
    Mizuko Wakabayashi (age 10), *12 months of training*

12. **Concerto No. 2** ....Seitz
    Toshihide Doi (age 7), *14 months of training*

13. **Perpetual Motion** ....Karl Böhm
    Teru Yasuda (age 7), *15 months of training*

14. **Aucassin et Nicolette**...Kreisler
    Jen Ch'eng-i (age 11), *1 1/2 years of training*

15. **Sonata No. 3, Allegro**...Handel
    Yasuko Okumura (age 11), *1 1/2 years of training*

16. **Concerto in A Minor**...Vivaldi
    Masaki Ikuta (age 7), *1 year and 8 months of training*

17. **Concerto in A Minor**...Vivaldi
    Nobumi Nakazato (age 11), *1 1/2 years of training*

18. **Concerto in A Minor**...Bach
    Masumi Kurosawa (age 7), *2 years of training*

19. **La Folia**........................Corelli
    Kenji Kobayashi (age 9), *2 years of training*

20. **Sonata No. 4** ....Handel
    Yoko Arimatsu (age 8), *2 1/2 years of training*

21. **The Rain**
    (Perpetual Motion)...........Karl Böhm
    Takeshi Kobayashi (age 11), *2 years of training*

22. **Concerto No. 5, A Major**.......Mozart
    Yoko Ishikawa (age 8), *4 years of training*

23. **Rondo** ....Mozart/Kreisler
    Koji Toyota (age 9), *5 1/2 years of training*

24. **Chaconne** ....Vitali/Charlier
    Miyo Ohta (age 13), *5 years of training*

The third concert program also lists the age and years of training of the children. Those who had heard them the year before could appreciate the children's progress in the last year.

For those who know the levels of the pieces, it should be easy to trace the children's leaping progress within one year. Although it may be too much to expect the same from people at large, I give the above as reference material anyway. This program took place in the fall four years ago. I discontinued instruction two years ago when I moved out of Tokyo. Two years after this program, Koji Toyota had developed enough to play the Beethoven Concerto; Yoko Ishikawa, the Mendelssohn Concerto; Miyo Ohta and Kenji Kobayashi, Bach's Chaconne; and Yoko Arimatsu and Takeshi Kobayashi the Vitali Chaconne.

"What superior ability shown by children," I marveled while instructing them. Since my principle is to let all of my young disciples participate in the concert, I did not have only champions perform. Many children had joined during the two years after the above concert so that I instructed about fifty children altogether.

Anyway, the ability demonstrated in the above program is the joyful product of an innovation in the teaching method I had tried since becoming aware of children's ability in speech. The ability the children demonstrated in the two years after this concert, I believe, surpassed the cultural standard of children in the world. It was indeed a pleasure for me to see that these children were showing accomplishments not inferior to those demonstrated in Hochschule graduation recitals I had heard in Berlin.

Here I think I need to say one thing. Since I insist that every child is capable, many questions naturally arise: what about children's innate traits? Aren't there differences in children's ability? Doesn't genius exist?

Needless to say, there are innate differences among children, and therefore naturally there are differences in their ability. Some people start from this fact and suggest working toward superiority through improving genes. This may certainly be a big issue, but it is a question of heredity, not of education, which is what I am discussing here.

I insist that children are capable. Starting out with the realization of their ability demonstrated in speech, I came to gain sufficient confidence to present it, for I have experienced the fact that their ability can develop beautifully in another area by improving instruction or educational approach. It is possible that it is due to my immature instruction that children have not yet in fact developed the same degree of ability as in speech. Imagine how wonderful it would be if a better approach were discovered, enabling children to develop the same degree of ability as they demonstrate in speech, or even more ability.

To those people who insist that children who can express themselves fluently are "incapable," let me say that I am convinced that I can help them so that they will not be called incapable. Having erred in educational approach and created nearly "incapable" children, teachers and parents stamp them as lacking in ability. I think present-day society badly errs in its understanding. Instead of being obsessed by innate traits, society should change its understanding and make efforts to raise every seed until it grows fine blossoms and fruit.

Therefore, the very concept of special approaches - say, early education or genius education - is already flawed. Unless the early education which I advocate comes to be understood as "general education," we do not yet have a correct concept of education. The ability of children fussed about as prodigies should be understood as normal ability, which every Japanese of tomorrow will demonstrate. In advancing national education, we must understand that this is no dream but something we can be expected to carry out. Let me repeat: I have come to think that the ability currently regarded as average may in fact be the lowest level of ability humans can demonstrate.

The number of children I have taught in the past dozen or so years may total one hundred. Among the nearly fifty students I was teaching at the time I left Tokyo, the following children either came to be known in today's musical circles or belonged to Group I (the highest group in my class): Itoko Hoshiide, Toshiya Eto, Keiko Yamamoto, Nakajima Ono, Nejiko Suwa (who first studied with Mogilevsky), Koji Toyota, Miyo Ohta, Yoko Ishikawa, Akihiko Aoki, Noriko Inaba, Kenji Kobayashi, Takeshi Kobayashi, Yoko Armatsu, Masumi Kurosawa, among others - they were all diligent workers, and each had the ability to demonstrate his or her own beautiful musical sensibility. They are outstanding people fostered at various periods of the last ten or so years of my teaching.

If my teaching lasts ten more years, more and more younger students will advance to Group I. In other words, the first ten years are the initial stage, and the number of students is also limited. Among this small class, many such capable students as cited above appeared one by one and made it possible for me to believe that, with the number of students increasing today, in the next decade several times more students will be fostered to the level of Group I. So, under my instruction alone, in the next ten years about one hundred students will one by one demonstrate Group I ability.

If the method of ability development is studied in each field, if many teachers instruct small children from their own specialist viewpoints in different areas of the country, and make efforts to foster superior ability, in the next ten years tens of thousands of children will be raised with outstanding strength. If such an era arrives, superior ability will shine throughout the nation, and eventually a country with a high level of cultural ability will be constructed.

Look at our country's musical circles today. If you omit from the list of famous performers all of those who received early education, what will remain? The results of early education carried out in the past dozen or so years are already a light in today's musical circles, and they maintain the height of Japan's musical culture, and provide hope for tomorrow. People have started to say in recent years that music training has to start in childhood. These words have come to be heard often because those who received early education have begun to demonstrate their outstanding strength in a striking way in musical circles.

If people's recognition has reached this point, we must advance this idea one more step. In other words, people have to become aware that *music is but one area of demonstrating human ability* and know that children have this strength in every area. It must be advocated by many people that human ability has to start being fostered in childhood.

In order for this to happen, early education has to be vigorously carried out not only in music but in general education so that many children will start to demonstrate their great ability. When this comes to pass, people will say that human ability has to start being fostered in childhood. Regrettably, however, it is extremely difficult to prove this as long as today's education system, with its sole emphasis on elementary school, is strictly observed. Therefore there seems to be no other way to prove this except in the areas of art.

The record for early education in my class is Koji Toyota, who, at two years and five or six months of age, played Dvořák's "Humoresque" when I held a student recital at the Japan Youth Hall in Tokyo. That a child can do this much if you let him at two years and five or six months indicates that there is much to be studied about early education. It is quite wrong to see the meaning of early education in the pleasure adults take when young children learn advanced things. The point is to what degree people who received skillful early education can demonstrate their ability in their maturity. *The strength the child will demonstrate throughout his life without relaxing his efforts when he grows up* - this ought to be the purpose of early education.

Therefore we must be careful that we do not blindly advocate early education, break records in early education, and help demonstrate outstanding ability only in early childhood. Otherwise, children will follow the saying "Divine at ten, average at twenty." The reason that children reputed to be divine become persons with average strength at twenty is because they go off the track once they are called divine, and the same effort and skillful instruction fail to continue until age twenty. Since I do not approve of the heartlessness of people who spread the rumor that a child is a "genius," I insist that "there are no geniuses," making myself the target of my friends' vigorous criticisms. However, the title of genius should be given after one's life is over when one's ability is evaluated; misled by the concept of the inborn, people make a fuss about a "genius" child who has demonstrated a little ability, and parents are so pleased that they go off the track along with the child.

According to a learned person, by age seven ordinary children know three to four thousand words. If this ability in the one area called speech grows in every child in seven years, and if ability is fostered in another area under the same superior instruction as in speech, children's ability can be raised to the level of speech. For example, if writing were taught so that children could fluently write three thousand symbols, we would be able to view it as ability which corresponds to their strength in speech.

In brief, the problem is nothing more than that *ability is not created because it is not fostered.* Japan should become a cultured nation which will foster children's ability to the level of their speech.

It has been discussed and is now about to be decided that, since we have too many characters, we should limit the number in use to fifteen hundred or two thousand.[2] This is one aspect, one problem, of what is advocated in present-day Japan with a people whose level of ability has become low. There also seem to be a considerable number of people who favor Romaji, or the romanized way of writing, instead of using Chinese characters and Japanese script. This, too, is a question we must deeply ponder. These ideas, stemming only from practicality, will turn into an enterprise which greatly lessens Japanese people's ability. This resembles the idea that since advanced math is complicated and aimlessly strenuous, with no direct relation to daily life, and taxes people to have to consume useless energy, we should abolish advanced math in the future. When reducing the number of Chinese characters or romanizing Japanese writing is discussed from the standpoint of the people's ability, it should be recognized that this will clearly result in retrogression of Japanese people's ability.

The written language cannot be expected to develop to a degree which the people's ability can no longer sustain. As cultural ability develops, written language advanced, too, requiring more and more complex and high-level expression. Since the level of ability of the Japanese people is not going to be the same in the future as it is today, there is no need to artificially and forcefully limit it now. Particularly if written Japanese is romanized, the people's ability will show signs of irreparable regression in a matter of twenty or thirty years. Conversely, supposing the Japanese writing system to be the most convenient, if England and the United States abolished the roman alphabet to switch to the Japanese system, what would happen? By this change, would English and American people take a long stride toward cultural progress? Or would they experience regression in ability? Unless everything is looked at from the standpoint of the nation's demonstration of ability, our views will tend to become myopic. The result is that such sad and odd topics begin to be

[2] Written Japanese consists of *kanji,* or Chinese characters, which are predominantly ideographs, and *kana,* which are phonetic symbols. Approximately 3,000 characters were in common use until 1946, when the number of Chinese characters for daily use became limited to 1,850 (later expanded to 1,945 characters). Elementary school children learn 880 of them.

seriously discussed as that too many *kanji* cause Japan's culture to stagnate, or that, Japanese culture will greatly advance if written Japanese is romanized, because it is cumbersome.

When I read *kanshi* poems (classical Chinese poetry, or poems written by Japanese in the same manner) by the fighters who played leading roles in the Meiji Restoration (1868), I am reminded that once young men in their twenties were able to compose and write beautifully such fine pieces with ink and brush. How many people in their twenties now have the ability to read them and compose equally fine poems? Can we say that Japanese have advanced culturally when we have regressed in literature from the standard which people demonstrated in the past? We are gradually lowering our own cultural standard in search of the simpler and more convenient. This can be considered proof of the fact that on the whole the Japanese have unawares been inviting the regression of ability. Human ability can develop endlessly if polished, while it can degrade itself in a brief period of time if simplicity is sought in rejection of what appears difficult.

I seem to have digressed quite a bit. At any rate, we must continue to study the question of the ability children demonstrate in speech, and try to establish a correct path for carrying out our important mission of developing the Japanese people's ability. This is the first issue we must address today.

BUDDING TALENT AND CHARACTER EDUCATION

It is a truth that a seed unplanted never grows. When I observe the different ways in which children's ability grows, it appears to me that the conditions for the growth of ability are not at all different from those of grass and trees.

Ability, like a seed, does not sprout unless there is stimulation. Some time ago I read a newspaper report about the discovery of 3,000-year-old cedar seeds, which, when planted, sprouted. It is the same with children's ability: it remains a seed forever if left alone without such necessary stimulation as soil, water and sun. Initial stimulation is likewise essential for the growth of every ability.

We often see a mother holding a baby and talking to him, saying "Pretty, pretty," pointing at flowers or toys, or repeating "Yum, yum" as she shows him food. Using many different words, she patiently talks to the baby every day again and again no matter how indifferent he is. To an outside observer, this repetition may seem totally wasteful. However, this is an important stimulus for developing the talent of speech in the baby, an important job like the daily watering, sunning, and fertilizing of the plants to bring them to sprout. This can be said not only about the sprouting of the ability to talk but about everything. One of my younger brothers often played beautiful recorded music for his baby. Perhaps the baby began to love music while this was repeated every day, for, even when she was crying, she would stop crying when the record was put on and would soon sleep peacefully. She became an easy baby who did not trouble her parents. Though just a baby, she seemed attracted to beautiful music and stayed quiet whenever a record was on. When she was a little older, she started to sing earlier than other children her age, and correctly.

Since the conditions are the same whether one helps ability or grass seeds to sprout, it is no good to stop in the middle after starting to foster ability. If one plants a seed, waters and suns it once or twice, then leaves it alone until the soil dries up, its sprouting will be delayed, or, in some cases, it will die. It is the same with speech. If repeated stimulation is given every day, the child never fails to learn to talk. This is confirmed by the fact that the length of time it takes before a child starts to talk differs from child to child depending upon the total environment.

Consider the situation found within families. Compared with the firstborn, those born later start to talk sooner - and the youngest begins earliest. Those who have two or three children must surely have observed this. This is the nature of the germination of ability. Therefore it is rash to decide that children who start to talk early are brighter than those who start late.

Thus, it is true that ability, in order to sprout, requires the important condition called *stimulation,* and that the amount of stimulation affects the timing of sprouting. Even in the period of germination there are differences in growth; but it is obvious that later, at the seedling stage, even more pronounced differences surface depending upon the instructor's skill and the learner's effort.

Therefore, we should first study the problem of instructive skill and hardworking *character.* Saving the aspect of instructive skill, or ability development, for a later chapter, I would first like to discuss my view of effort, or diligence.

On comparing my more than fifty young students with sundry abilities, I observe a variety of characters. Those who are responsive and hardworking always stride ahead. Discovering this fact through actually teaching them, I thought I must inquire into how a child's hardworking character is created. In other words, I began to think about whether character is inborn or created through education. This is directly related to success in children's ability development: if hardworking responsive character can be created, the task of fostering children's ability will become easy.

With this view in mind, I did my best to observe possible causative factors from which children's character derives. As a result, I arrived at this conclusion: character is not innate; like ability it is fostered from infancy through daily life, stimulation, environment, training, instruction, and so on.

If someone for no particular reason repeatedly snatches away what is in a baby's hand, the baby will become alert and start to strongly resist letting go. After he has grown a little more, he will have learned to hide cookies behind his back.

As he behaves this way again and again, it will become part of his nature. In a family with many children, the firstborn, whether boy or girl, is likely to be raised with care and to develop a responsive nature, whereas the youngest siblings, especially if they are close together in age, often need to protect their things from big brothers, consequently developing a totally different character.

"Why are they so different if they are siblings?" This is a comment I often hear. Raised by the same parents and going to the same school, siblings tend to develop completely different personalities - this may be incomprehensible even to the parents themselves. Think about it, though. Suppose there are two brothers. The oldest brother was at first solely under his parents' influence, while the environment in which a second son was raised included the parents and the big brother, who was sometimes unreasonable. It is only natural that widely different characters have developed. Further, I feel that the character created and developed in early childhood exerts powerful influence even after the child is grown, as if it is his inborn nature which cannot be discarded. Similarly, if a little pine tree growing on a windy beach is transplanted to a quieter environment, the trunk of the pine, twisted by the strong wind, can never be straightened, and even after full growth the tree will retain an image of its old crooked self. What nature demonstrates can be said of personality developed in human childhood. The qualities fostered through stimulation in infancy and childhood contribute to shape the child's personality and affect his entire future. Since those with a hardworking nature can demonstrate their real strength through hard work, they succeed in whatever work they undertake.

If they realize this, parents should no longer be able to lazily neglect children's character and ability, ascribing them as in the past to the children's inborn nature. I would like people to make new their observations and judgments concerning this important question which affects children's entire lives.

From long ago it has been said that "mixing with red turns one red." As white paper is dyed by any color, children absorb and reflect everything with which they come into contact. Even complex, multicolored parts of the environment are projected in their different colors, creating a child's character that is thought to be his original nature or inborn quality.

When one realizes this, character education is understood to be no more a matter of theory; it makes no sense merely to explain it and have it mentally understood. For example, even if you tell a child a hundred or a thousand times not to be unkind, what will happen if his parents and siblings live their daily lives contrary to these words and expose him to unkind deeds? Or if their friends act unkindly to this young child? Their behavior may contribute to his character formation with stimuli tens and hundreds of times stronger than those words. The spiritual world shared by the family at home, especially the members' language and behavior, is reflected in the child, dyeing him and forming his character. Through observing a large number of children, I feel convinced that this is an immutable truth. It is awesome that the process starts in infancy.

At present spiritual education is all too verbal and theoretical; there is a popular trend to emphasize words and sentences and expect results, but if having children read for mental comprehension were really effective, the book-reading country Japan should have long been filled with people of a beautiful heart and beautiful character. How can we evaluate our present society? Millions of good books and incessant advice have scattered like rain in the past and present. Yet humanity is straying farther and farther away from beautiful hearts, beautiful life.

Regarding character education, I think we should start to give more direct, truthful education in our daily lives.

There are examples of living things that completely change their appearances and habits in response to environmental changes. A salamander called *axolotl,* which lives in high plateaus in Mexico, was originally a water animal and breathes through the gills like a fish. When left out of water, it is said to change into an *ambystoma* resembling a newt. Again, a king of water flea called *artemia* (brine shrimp) is, I hear, transformed into a totally different being called *branchiopod* when the salt content of the water is reduced. These examples are suggestive of how children's character is formed, though invisibly, through interaction with the environment; they hint that surprising changes can occur in a child's character depending upon education.

Kiso Fukushima, where I live at present, is a town in the Kiso mountains. So there are many tree connoisseurs. Looking at a log or a board, they can tell with precision what kind of tree, what mountain and what area it comes from; which side faced east and which side faced south, north, or west; and what its quality is as wood. The reason that they can tell these things is that even in the same kind of tree there are differences in the color of the wood and the texture of the grain, depending on the soil. The way the year rings are formed tells the direction of the wind and sun, and the quality of the wood and shapes of the rings make it possible to imagine the valley where the tree grew. A child's character, too, is nurtured under sundry influences according to his home and other environments. If one watches carefully, one can judge, by everything that a child is, the lives and personalities of his parents, as well as the family's surroundings.

As noted above, "Those who mix with red turn red." Babies are like white paper which is gradually dyed diverse colors through contact with the environment. The ability and character of us who have already grown seems to be like paper which has been dyed and stained in many different - and, moreover, fairly dark - colors over a long period of time. Although it has been two years since I came to Kiso and I can understand Kiso dialect, I can hardly imitate its delicate characteristics or its accent, cadence, and intonation skillfully. However, my younger brother's six-year-old child has completely switched to Kiso dialect, effortlessly reproducing its intonation and other subtle aspects.

This means that I, no longer a white piece of paper, have duller ability to learn language, while the child, still close to the white paper state, is freely dyed in the color of Kiso dialect. The closer one is to the white paper state, the sharper one's sensitivity to colors, and the clearer the results one gets from dyeing. Adults like us, who have already been dyed in multifarious hues, cannot hope for white paper's sensitivity; since we are already in the state of a dirty finish, which can be further colored only by exceptionally strong dyes, our sensitivity is extremely dull whether in ability or character. This suggests how important early education is.

To give another example, many people have experienced the difficulty of speaking a foreign language: going abroad at a mature age, they place themselves in the daily environment of a foreign language and study it, yet their ability to speak that language remains so limited that it cannot begin to compare with their fluency in Japanese. With still older people, the dyeing is even darker, and their progress is worse than ours. The younger people are, the sharper their sensitivity in both talent and character. Carefully watch children who accompany their parents abroad and are raised there: they have fine pronunciation no different from that of children of that land. The children learn to speak the language with an accent that is far more genuine than that which their parents can ever acquire.

That children, compared with adults, demonstrate superior absorption of and sensitivity to language indicates that the same is true in the area of character. Flawed education in that period can create worse results than adults think; it is scary. As a person grows, he gradually develops a fixed character, but his character in childhood was not yet so clear. The closer to infancy the child is, the less defined the character. It is obvious that character changes in many ways through contact with the environment.

In early childhood, when sensitivity and absorption are powerful, *the very best educational opportunity, which will never return again,* occurs. Whether to develop character or ability, educators and parents must clearly and consciously understand that they should pour their energy in this period into education, which is never to be neglected.

Willfulness

I have already stated that the character dyed into the child plays a big role in developing ability. For example, children who are uncontrollably willful develop ability slowly. In order to develop their children's ability smoothly, parents must make an effort not to raise willful children. A willful child starts something and is immediately bored, for that is his character. So he abandons what he does not like, seeking something else. In many cases, the parent, loving the child in the wrong way, flatters the child too much, unintentionally allowing him to talk and behave as willfully as he wants. In the end, even the parent does not know what to do. Moreover, if this is not corrected, the child becomes a lazy person with neither self-reflection nor calmness, who, although speaking like a full-fledged adult, cannot carry out and complete a single thing.

In order to save the child from such an outcome, it is quite effective to help him concentrate on one thing. This is so important that it is the first condition of ability development.

At the same time, it is an exercise in gradually training his easily bored heart, engaging him in one thing, forming good character, and changing his future for the better. A friend's wife always gave one toy to their child, refraining from giving him another until it broke. This is a wise approach. When you show another toy to a child holding one, he throws the one he has aside and tries to get the new one. If he eyes still another toy, he immediately craves that one. Finally, such a character is formed in him that he seeks any new thing, without distinguishing between good and poor. Moreover, he will cry if he does not get what he wants; so you give it to him. He learns this sly technique of crying to get something, and he cries the moment you say something to him. Since it cannot be helped, you give him whatever he wants. In the end he cries although he no longer knows what he wants. The situation is so helpless that it is almost as if crying is his job. At this point, it is too late. A newborn cannot know such a technique; the parent has guided the baby to become willful in this way. Willfulness starts in infancy. If parents pay attention to this matter and grasp children's psychology from infancy, they should be able to induce them naturally to grow with an easy, responsive character. In many cases, children of wealthy families are so spoiled that they are lazy and whimsical, and stop halfway no matter what they start to do. They tend to grow as people with no strong points. This is because they are given whatever they want and are helped to develop an easy-to-be-bored character before they know it. So many families create this result from indulging their children too much.

My younger brother laughingly told me the other day about his boy who is about two years and six months old. He was at play in the yard when he stumbled on something and fell, and cried loudly. Hearing this, his mother opened a sliding paper door and found nothing alarming. "You're a good boy. Get on your feet by yourself," she said, but he remained crying, refusing to rise. "If you fall, you must pick yourself up at once," she said again. Since the boy did not rise, she closed the sliding door as before. When she peered through the slit between the doors, she saw that he eventually stopped crying, rose, and walked toward the door. Then he slid open one of the doors, saw his mother's face, went back to where he had been, tumbled over, and cried. She closed the door again. After this was repeated three times, the child gave up, stopped crying, and came back to the room.

The above story shows child psychology which makes one smile, portraying the lovely way a child covets his mother's attention. However, the mother ought not to succumb. This is indeed a childlike demonstration, the message being "Lift me." Even such a small event can suggest how different character traits are formed in daily life.

A German once said to me, "Japan is children's paradise." This is a sharp comment which satirizes Japanese children's upbringing. He probably thought that Japanese parents have no understanding of child education, leaving children alone to be as willful as they want. In trains and on streets, he must have often seen mothers at a loss, defeated by their children's willfulness. There is no limit to the willfulness that may develop if you leave your child alone as he becomes willful and continues to behave as his heart desires. It is up to the mother to educate the child skillfully so that he will not be like that.

Control yourself - to form the habit of sacrificing one's desire and making efforts is the first lesson that the parent must teach the child. Whether in talent education or humanity education, this is where the road branches off, either to success or to failure. Ninomiya Sontoku[3] says:

> Few people clearly understand the difference between natural logic and the human way. If there are human bodies, there is greed. This is natural logic. It is the same as that weeds grow on the farm. Dikes collapse, moats bury themselves, and bridges rot - these represent natural logic. Now, the way of humans is in controlling egoism; the way is in weeding on the farm, the way is in repairing dikes, cleaning moats, and replacing old bridges with new ones.

> Heaven's logic and the human way being thus separate, heaven's logic is eternally invariable, while the human way decays if neglected even one day. Therefore, the human way is worthy when discipline is applied; it is not when left alone. Discipline desired for the way of humans is in the teaching of self-control. The self means egoism. Egoism can be compared to a weed in the field. Control means to pull out the weed growing in the field, while "self-control" means to shave off and throw away the weed growing in the field of one's own heart, letting the rice and barley of one's mind thrive. This is called the way of humans. When Confucius says, 'Control the self and return to the rites,' he means this discipline.

I think this is a golden saying. We must not only savor these words and try to practice the way but recognize this as an objective more important than anything else in children's character education.

Willfulness represents egoism, the weed Master Sontoku talks about. Unless parents quickly take away this weed, there is no way rice and barley can grow in children's hearts. If you pay close attention in daily life from early on, pull out weeds until you see a beautiful field of grain, and thus guide your child's character in a good direction; then afterward rice and barley should grow well on their own. If you leave the field alone two, or even three years, letting the weed called willfulness grow as it likes, how can you expect to see it turn into a beautiful farm?

Master Sontoku's golden saying teaches us adults to have discipline, and at the same time is a truly fine lesson for parents raising children. Self-control is the way of humans; at the

[3.] Ninomiya Sontoku (1787–1856) was a late Edo agronomist who restored many abandoned farm villages and opened new lands. He advocated virtue, goodness, frugal living, and diligence. Ninomiya is his family name, Sontoku his pen name; he is also known by his childhood name, Kinjiro.

same time, it is discipline which, with each swing of the spade, cultivates one's future in a positive direction. Creating self-control in such a way that it becomes part of the child's character is the parent's supreme gift for the child.

I have explained the need for early correction of the child's willfulness, which should not be left alone. In actuality, there are many different approaches: some will try to weed the child's field by scolding him; others will skillfully attract the child's interest in order to correct willfulness indirectly. Those who carefully raise children by weeding willfulness skillfully in daily life from their infancy are the greatest experts; and this method is the least painful.

Next, although this may be somewhat difficult when the child is already three or four, since by then the weed has grown quite tall, correction is still possible by giving a child talent education: teach one specific thing to a child and train him to concentrate on that single thing. This is the second method. The worst approach is to try to correct the child's weakness and willfulness by scolding. The parent is responsible if the child is already willful. The child cannot understand verbal explanation; if he is suddenly scolded for doing what he has been permitted to do until now, he cannot be expected to understand it. It is quite difficult to correct what has long been a habit, and it is a big mistake to simply scold, thinking that the child will not repeat the error if badly scolded. You must understand that it takes three years of remedial work to correct the character formed in three years, and must be prepared patiently and repeatedly to guide and teach the child. In any case, you ought to know that raising your child with willfulness represents the failure of character education.

Here I would like to add an explanation of the corrective method I use in violin instruction. The primary job of violin instruction is to correct students' weak points. As weaknesses are eliminated, naturally a child gradually improves and becomes a better player. The following is the method I use in correcting students.

When I give a lesson to a student, I first have him play for me, and I pay attention to the various defects in his performance. There may be errors in the playing technique, problems of musical expression, flaws in posture, or mistakes in the method of practice. Most students manifest over a dozen diverse shortcomings. While the student plays, I keep thinking about the most serious shortcoming he must correct.

There are different degrees of weak points: like fingers, some are long and others are short, all on display there. So, I endeavor to discover the gravest of his faults, or the middle finger, so to speak, which is the longest among the fingers. When I recognize it as a key weakness, I set to correcting that single point. Therefore, my lesson concentrates on determining the greatest defect at the moment and *correcting that single defect.* In every lesson, I assign the student to work at home on just one defect and show him how to correct it. If the weakness is not yet corrected by the next lesson, I do not let him advance but point out the same thing, and with sufficient explanation give the same assignment to take home. Until this most serious shortcoming is corrected, I refuse to point out the next shortcoming, and make the student work on correction of that single weakness.

Let me give you an extreme example. A music school student, though unusually diligent, was unaware of a grave defect in his string playing method. At each lesson I pointed it out, explained it, and worked toward correcting it; but, perhaps because he was lacking in the desire to explore, the student failed to correct it. I knew that he would never be able to produce beautiful tone or improve technically as long as he failed to correct that defect, so every lesson was on that single point alone. Since I patiently persisted in what I believed, nearly one year was consumed on that point alone. Still he did not try to correct his fault. I said to him: "Since you have made no effort to accept my advice and explanation for the past year relating to your biggest defect, my lessons are now meaningless. This is your last lesson with me. However, if you go home today and seriously try to ponder what I have talked about for one year, I will listen to you once more after one week. Everything will be decided then. If you still do not correct yourself, I will decline to teach you, and process your withdrawal from school."

A week passed after this ultimatum. When the student came to my room and played, his weakness had suddenly been fixed. His tone was consequently more beautiful, and his technique had progressed. Probably he was shocked enough by the ultimatum to think seriously about how to correct himself and practice toward that end. In other words, he woke from the illusion of the foolish idea that one improves if one merely makes efforts, and finally realized that the path for true improvement was *to explore what is correct and to actively train in it.* After the event, the student made rapid progress, and continued to correct himself according to my instruction, responsively and quickly.

When, in this manner, a student does his best to correct the biggest defect, and that defect becomes small, the second biggest defect begins to stand out. When the second defect becomes small, the third defect is ready to be corrected. Thus my instruction is always given step-by-step; I never point out all the defects in one lesson, nor try to correct two or three defects at the same time. As in eliminating the weak point of the first joint of the index finger after correcting the weak point of the first joint of the middle finger after correcting the first joint of the index finger, I endeavor to make the shape of the mountain smooth. Thus, I adopted the method of gradually eliminating current defects one by one; after I adopted this method, my disciples' progress became quite remarkable.

I have described my corrective approach for your reference. I think it most effective to apply such a method to children's character education and to guide them through one thing at a time.

Next is the question of creating diligent character. Hard work is the base of a child's life-work. In talent education, too, diligence determines success. In order to guide a child toward diligence, it is ineffective to explain diligence verbally or to try to command him. The parent must start instruction by doing the activity together with the child, while experiencing such joy as is felt by a child at play. Moreover, it has to be repeated daily for the sake of the child, even if for only five minutes each time, until it becomes a habit. This is the way to create character.

In a certain family, although they have one or two employees, four children clean the corridors with wet cloth every morning before going to school, everyone working on a fixed allotted area. All four do it at the same time happily as if at play. The mother does her share together with the children. The children delightedly run around, each cleaning his area, which takes only five or ten minutes. The youngest child, five or six years old, copies the older ones and goes around wiping the floor, chuckling. This is a truly active few minutes, and it is a moment when fresh morning air fills the house.

Now, if the mother tells the oldest child to do it alone, joy cannot be created. Joy is born where everyone works together, even if for five minutes, so that the youngest child runs around having fun like the others. In other words, this is the knack of character education: diligence must be cultivated as daily habit so that it is a joy. If there is liveliness in the house, the child spontaneously copies only the cheerful, active aspects of family life. The true reflection of this is witnessed after the child is grown, when it bears real fruit.

The story of the mother of Mencius (a Chinese philosopher and disciple of Confucius), who moved three times to assure that he received good education, is a good example of how environment affects the child's character. However, the more direct influence on a child's character education comes from the family itself and the child's friends. Therefore, no matter how many times one moves after the example of Mencius' mother, it only ends in farce if the family itself is no good. First, family; second, friends. It is imagined that the primary reason why Mencius' mother moved might have been his friends.

As an old saying has it, "Let your child board at another's house." This is a good way to eliminate the weed called willfulness. Those who do not find it strenuous to control the self and make efforts are diligent, hardworking and capable of self-reflection. So they can become people who succeed no matter what they do. Behind success in the world, there is always self-control and diligence, without which fine achievement cannot be expected.

HOW TO FOSTER ABILITY

What are the conditions and kind of guidance under which ability develops? I would like to record what I learned through my experience. The most important points for fostering ability, or letting human ability manifest itself, follow.

To begin, the instructor must thoroughly understand the two approaches to education: *to teach and advance,* and *to foster ability with attention to its gradual increase.* It is necessary to clearly distinguish between these completely different ways of teaching.

Teaching and advancing is an approach that the instructor can modify in any way he wishes. Whether the student does or does not understand the content, the instructor can let him advance rapidly so that the reins of progress are completely in the hands of the instructor. On the other hand, the *gradual reinforcement of ability* brings about changes in the strength of the instructed. This changing strength is precisely the ability that the instructor must carefully foster. It is crucial that the instructor, recognizing the distinction between these two points, tries to instruct with careful attention to *how ability is reinforced.* Although this may seem all too obvious, few in fact give successful instruction recognizing the distinction.

Simple as it is when summarized like this, in actual practice this problem is related to the instructor's quality of and skill in instruction and makes a great difference in the demonstration of the student's power as the result of instruction. Therefore, even an instructor with superior ability can instruct without much effect if he lacks understanding of this point, while an instructor who understands this, though of inferior ability, can produce much better students. Here is the basis for the distinction between so-called skillful and clumsy teachers. Here too is the answer to the question: Why is that teacher with great ability so poor at teaching? That kind of teacher, since he is capable himself, tends to rapidly *teach and advance* students, assuming that they understand the material taught to a certain degree, and ends up being the clumsiest instructor.

Such is the difference between the teach-and-advance approach and the develop-the-ability approach. It is the clumsy teacher who thinks, as is commonly thought, that when the student understands the material, the teacher's duty is over and it is time to go on to the next lesson. Let me give an example in musical instruction of how many instructors teach. Suppose an instructor teachers Mozart's Turkish March in piano. The student finally learns to play the piece after several lessons, and now can play it by heart for the teacher. Both teacher and student think that the piece has been taught and learned. The teacher assigns a new piece; the student is happy to study it because he not only has learned one piece but has advanced to the next. However, since this is done from the standpoint of instruction which *teaches and advances,* it is difficult for the student to develop his ability.

It is the same in math or language. Suppose the instructor gives a problem and explains it, and the student understands the explanation, and proves capable of handling the problem without a mistake. This may be interpreted as perfect comprehension, and the student may be advanced to the next stage. If so, this is the same as the above case in piano, a clumsy instruction which *teaches and advances*. To cite another similar example, suppose the action of throwing and catching a ball constitutes a lesson. The teacher explains to the child how to throw and catch a ball, then lets him throw and catch it as practical training. The above kind of instruction is the same as considering the learning completed when the child can now throw and catch the ball. This is the degree of instruction of those who think instruction involves only teaching and advancing. However, from the viewpoint of what strength a child can develop through this, the result is miserable, for the only thing gained is knowledge.

At this rate, what happens to the development of ability the person should be capable of demonstrating? For example, the agility children show in baseball, the human ability exemplified by their precision in pitching and catching - aren't these examples of great strength overlooked by instructors who think that to instruct is to *teach and advance?* What I call instruction is the fostering of true human ability, which the children are expected to demonstrate. Although the above example may not be adequate, I gave it because it is the most obvious. What underlies the best instruction can be found in children's *language learning.* It can be observed before our eyes every day.

Why can children learn to speak so fluently? Isn't it because the teaching method in speech is the supreme method that every child demonstrates this human ability so beautifully? I would like to describe the method based on this idea, by which I succeeded in instruction and helped children demonstrate their ability beautifully.

As I said before, in most music instruction, when a student can play a piece by heart in front of the teacher, the piece is regarded as finished and the student advances to the next level. However, I regard this level of playing a piece from memory as the *lowest level of ability.* Hence, my lesson starts when the student can play a piece from memory. My students always take my lesson without the music; I take the music, write in instructions in pencil, and return it. If the points remarked upon are corrected well by the next lesson, I erase those instructions before returning the music, but the points not corrected remain as part of the assignment.

Thus, I instruct the student so that his performance will be more secure and more beautifully expressive lesson by lesson, and train and correct him until his performance approaches my goal, that is, a great master's performance which I have in my mind.

I do this from the beginner stage, the injunction to "teach beginners like beginners" does not exist in my instruction. Even at the beginner stage, when a child can play a piece, I train and correct him so that he can play it more beautifully and with greater ease. Only here the demonstration of human ability starts; this is the method of fostering ability.

Even a beginner learns to feel, in his own beginner way, that what seemed difficult to play at first is now an easy piece which he can play effortlessly. This is proof of real ability created. If we let the student always go through this stage, foster real ability, and skillfully guide him to the next stage while letting him feel it is easy, he will be able to gradually demonstrate human ability and reach a difficult stage which startles people, while finding the process always easy. Therefore, I think that instruction which makes "what is easy feel easy, what is difficult, difficult" is not yet thoroughgoing; instruction which can make "what is easy feel easy, what is difficult also feel easy" is truly skillful.

Advancing to a higher stage is, in general, the idea of progress; however, from the viewpoint of fostering ability, it cannot always be assumed to be so. Therefore, I always tell my students and their parents the following:

> What is most important is not the question of a high or low level. It is how accurately and how beautifully each student can play the piece he is learning at present. A less advanced student who plays well the less advanced piece he is assigned has a higher status than an advanced student who plays a difficult, high-level piece clumsily. We should respect *quality rather than quantity* from the viewpoint of human ability. Those who make efforts until they can play a piece well, even if a low-level piece, will some day be able to play high-level pieces beautifully.

When we look at the reality of current education in our country from this viewpoint, we realize that instruction that is shocking is given at many schools. No matter how many class hours are missed, some teachers try to rush the class to where they are supposed to be at the end of the school year, or try to advance to the next grade those children who do not even understand what is going on now at all, when it is obvious that the next grade will be more difficult. It is as if they believe that the Japanese can advance to a culturally higher level only if students are given graduation certificates. So much education is done in today's Japan which makes it difficult to judge the ability that educators aim to foster. At this rate a superior nation can in no way be created.

When the question of *instruction which helps demonstrate human ability* is thoroughly understood by many educators, and people understand that *teaching and advancing is a mere procedure of instruction,* education in our country will be transformed, instructional methods will improve, and many outstanding children will be fostered.

Next, I would like to state how important beginner stage instruction is in every area, and how much care should go into it. When first learning something, the child is in the pure white paper state, no ability having been developed. This applies to teaching adults also: there is no ability yet in that new area.

Instruction at this stage all the more requires patience and effort to foster the buds of talent. If instruction which *teaches and advances* is given, that instruction ends in total failure. Let me describe my class with young children.

On my teaching violin to three- or four-year olds, many comment: "How do you teach such small children? It must be quite painstaking." However, to me instructing children is far easier than instructing adults, they develop exactly as I wish, so it is not at all painstaking. Moreover, in the case of young children, rather than instructing the children, I teach their mothers the crux of instructing and correcting them. Of course many mothers neither know music nor play the violin. However, since they listen to me intently and help their children practice at home as I tell them, every child learns to play well in his own way. Children raised in different environments have different characters, and although they all become diligent students who play confidently in two or three years, at first they are really different.

One comes to my house, enters the lesson room, and after only a little while he insists on going home. Another listens quietly to other children's lessons as long as twenty or thirty minutes. Three-year-olds concentrate on one thing for only a very brief period of time, and hardly have any desire to play the violin. I start with them in this state. Therefore, if I teach the child to hold the bow in his right hand, then try to let him hold the violin in his left hand, his mind shifts to the violin and he drops the bow. If I first teach him to hold the violin in his left hand and then help him hold the bow in his right hand, the violin slips from his left hand. The first lesson ends here. It is impossible to teach more because his mind does not accept it.

Finally succeeding in letting him hold both the bow and the violin at the second lesson, I try to start letting him play one note, "Mother, a bird's flying," the child says, running toward the window, pointing at a bird outside; this concludes the second lesson. The child progresses more at the third lesson, holding the bow and violin and finally producing a sound once by rubbing a string. The moment this is done, "That's enough," he says, spoiling the lesson. This would probably make a third person feel impatient, but it is just fine like this.

It is natural that the bud of a child's ability starts to grow from this degree of preparation. Even if he produces only one sound, that the three lessons have helped him concentrate enough for his mind to focus on *playing* indicates great progress from the first lesson, and as long as there is this progress, this child will certainly be able to play some day. In half a year or so, a child of this level can confidently play a gavotte or a minuet at Hibiya Public Hall.

At the beginner stage, when the child is in the white paper state with no budding of ability, the instructor is required to use this much minute care and patience, for this is the stage where the child needs to be trained in what is proper and easy until he can do it well. If the bud of ability is fostered this way, ability gradually develops, and with the increase of ability, the speed of progress increases.

In whatever case, the instructor should always understand that the situation is exactly the same as with the baby beginning to learn to speak.

The beginning is like this in everything. It is important to think about how clumsy it is to rapidly advance in the material at this point. All children who hate math or cannot handle math, I believe, can be called victims of such clumsy instruction. "If they can do it, they learn to love it; if they cannot do it, they begin to hate it" - this is what the instructor should be aware of concerning ability development. Let children do only what they can do, train them until they can do it beautifully, and through this foster their ability. This ought to be one of the principles of teaching. It is not a question of levels. Let me summarize important points of instruction required for fostering human ability beautifully.

1. Since a beginner has not yet developed ability, use special care, and nurture the bud of talent by having him repeatedly practice what is easy until he can do it confidently. This is where the road divides between success and failure.

2. Always have the child train in what corresponds to the ability which is growing in him in such a way that he does not think it difficult.

3. In accordance with the developing ability, occasionally give such instruction as will induce the ability to grow faster and better through efforts.

4. Always help the child form a habit of making efforts until he can do the assignment in an accomplished way. Do not make allowance for the degree of the difficulty of the problem.

If you instruct and foster a child's ability upon fully understanding the above points, you will surely achieve good results, and superior human ability will be demonstrated.

Long ago I read in a book whose title I no longer recall that the training method for *ninja* in the old days included the exercise for learning the high jump: "Plant a young hemp, and jump over it every day."

This gave me a powerful suggestion. The way to create extraordinary human strength, I feel, is just as commonplace as this. It is said that hemp grows rapidly, but I am sure it grows steadily only to the eyes of one who watches its growth every day so that there is no remarkable difference between yesterday and today.

One who can jump over a foot long hemp today will surely be able to do so tomorrow. One who can jump over it tomorrow will certainly be able to jump over it the day after tomorrow. While this commonplace training is repeated fifty or sixty times daily with attention to correct posture and proper pacing, strength in the legs and good posture should gradually develop. While a clever method is followed of jumping easily every day over what one jumped over yesterday, the hemp grows ceaselessly and unnoticed.

By the time the hemp grows higher than human height, before he knows it the trainee has become a jumper who can easily jump over that tree through the daily accumulation and reinforcement of strength which has been developed up to that point. Developing this outstanding ability is the purpose of the training, and we should grasp many superior principles of instruction from this training method.

If the student skips practice and sits back, thinking that anyone can jump over a hemp which is now one-and-a-half feet tall, the strength which has been developing within him takes a rest, and with the rest regresses. Therefore, his ability does not grow parallel to the ceaseless growth of the tree, and as the tree grows to his height, it becomes difficult to jump over, and he fails in creating outstanding ability.

If he thinks it foolish to start daily training when the hemp is about one foot, and starts training with another hemp which he can comfortably jump over, he hardly has enough strength to catch up with its growth. Again, if unaware of the excellent conditions for training provided by a hemp plant, he daily trains with a stick or something, there will be a big difference in the growth of his ability in the end.

As indicated in the method of hemp jumping, the secret of instruction for the growth of ability is in grasping the great truth that human ability can be developed to an outstanding level through daily training by an extremely commonplace method. This should be called the crux of teaching.

THE POWER OF HABIT

The bud of ability grows with the help of the fertilizer called habit; the power of habit is the power which lets one's ability grow to the fullest. If this fertilizer is discontinued even for a while, ability becomes frail.

In my class, children come to take a lesson every third or fourth day. My request to their mothers is for an extremely brief practice session: "Please have your child practice ten minutes every day." If, according to her convenience, a mother skips the child's practice two days and brings him to the lesson after three days' worth of sudden and eager practice in thirty minutes, I can clearly see that two days were missed. There is a big difference between the strength developed through regular ten minutes of daily practice and that developed through sudden practice for half an hour on the third day. In other words, as I said before, skipping two days means two days of *negative growth* of strength. People do not notice that the child's ability is not so different after the third day's half hour practice from that of four days ago at the last lesson.

Human ability is strange. No matter how many times a student practices a difficult section where his fingers do not move as he wants because of lack of familiarity, he cannot master it if he tries it at the required tempo; all he accomplishes is to go helter-skelter. However, suppose he practices the section much slower than the required tempo, as though to tell it to the fingers, repeating it correctly twenty or thirty times. And suppose he drops it at that that day. When he plays it at the required speed right away on the following day, strangely he is now able to play correctly what he could not the day before. Even if the player has no confidence that he can play it, the fingers and the brain which formed the habit play it for him. When this practice method is applied to endeavors like violin study which require technique, it is so effective that it is almost amusing. Since this way of correctly forming a habit becomes the foundation of technical growth, those in all fields who are interested in technique ought to know its awe-inspiring power.

One condition necessary for ability development is that the student never fail to train repeatedly every day, even if briefly. If the session is longer, so much the better.

There are many examples of the awe-inspiring power of daily repeated training. We see in our daily lives children having fun playing catch every day. When they become skilled, they demonstrate wonderful, sophisticated ability, simple though the actions used in baseball and other games may be. That skill, too, is a result of successful development of one ability. Through daily training, children learn to measure the ball's speed, precise position, and distance. We must not underestimate children's brain function here but see that they develop that ability through having fun, naturally, and by the easiest method. This is a matter of training brain function; I am sure those skilled enough to become school baseball players will be useful people with well-functioning brains when they go out into society. One condition should be counted as a cause of such ability: *training students while helping them to feel interested.* In other words, at first the training may be other-inspired, but it becomes self-inspired once interest is stimulated, and the child does not spare any effort. Since he now finds pleasure in it on his own accord, he improves fast.

Whatever you have young children do, they are usually not too interested at first. If we eventually succeed in having them foster self-control with which they tell themselves that they must do it, they begin to take an interest in the learning, whether math or language, and this leads to *pride and joy of accomplishment.* Let a child do today what he did yesterday, and praise him if he does it well. Gradually it becomes easier for him, and the result is joy and pride. Guiding the student so that he himself becomes interested is one important method. A key point of instruction, it can therefore be said, is that interest springs out of confidence.

We all have experienced this. I remember being forced to think about difficult math problems in my elementary school days: I felt greatly tormented while staring at the blackboard and my notebook for five or ten minutes. When this kind of thing happens repeatedly, a child begins to lose patience in math little by little, ultimately turning into an irrecoverable math hater. So he achieves less and less. In present educational circumstances, millions of children are being victimized by such clumsy teaching.

"Let them think; it improves their brains" - this one-sided, mistaken view is what creates this kind of instruction. If the child forgets today what he learned yesterday, do not force him to think but teach it to him again immediately so he understands it, and repeat it again tomorrow and let him try it. This way, new understanding and ability are spontaneously added on, and the stage is soon reached where the child himself finds it fun. In order to develop ability, this method must be followed: from the beginner stage to a more difficult and higher level, avoid unpleasant, wasted hours or forced approaches, and form good habits until the child finds even a high-level assignment easy.

Let me repeat what I said before about habit: one has no ability yet when what is easy is felt to be easy and what is difficult is felt to be difficult. Ability has been created when, finding *what is easy, easy, and what is difficult, also easy,* the student can do it on the spot. It is here that the great power of habit manifests. Thus, I proceed with my students in such a way that the main emphasis is on letting them learn with ease, while I avoid forcing them. I instruct them while watching their real ability so as to advance them, before they know it, to a level which is generally thought high and difficult. Therefore, I think that the essential points in instruction are measuring the student's real ability, training and helping him form habits using materials appropriate to his level, and developing his real ability. To cite an extreme example of ability development, we find the following among experiments on instructing animals. If the instructional method is proper, such results seem possible.

Let me quote a passage from Dr. Chiyomatsu Ishikawa's book:

Another interesting thing here is language. So far, only human beings use language. Today no one questions the fact that language has an essential relationship to human development.

However, understanding language is not limited to human beings. From long ago, horses and dogs have often been said to understand human speech, although it was rather recently that this started being scientifically researched. It began in the late nineteenth century with the famous German horse called Hans. As everyone knows today, he had the ability to understand many words, and was also capable of doing fairly difficult calculations. Later it came to be known that, if taught, many other horses understood speech. Similar experiments conducted on dogs have clarified that they, too, have comprehension. One who is conducting particularly scholarly experiments on these animals is Dr. Tigrel of Stuttgart. I have written elsewhere about his work with dogs.

Thus, many cases of linguistic comprehension can be found in animals. They can also express words if only a method is taught; it is simply that they cannot utter them - although it is not that no animal has ever uttered a human word, either. Having studied the brains of apes, Bishop stated in 1876 that the orangutan had the most developed brain. Ten years ago Jacob and Onelli, who did profound studies of animal and human brains, also clarified that among apes the orangutan comes closest to the human brain. In a cage, the orangutan is less active than a chimpanzee, and hence may look denser, but that may be so for the very reason that the orangutan has a more developed intellect. In any case, all three frontal lobes are well developed in his brain. The third frontal lobe is said to be the linguistic center unique to human beings, but this, too, is developed to some extent. Therefore, if the orangutan does not talk, that is not because he lacks the linguistic center, or because he never thinks.

Thus, some animals comprehend speech, and of course think. The development of wisdom in animals like chimpanzees that are frequently experimented on is quite impressive, and in some aspects horses and dogs can be wiser than inferior human individuals. For example, while cases have been found among Australian aborigines of inability to count over five, some chimpanzees have been known to count over ten.

Hans, the horse, was able to count fairly complex numbers, and among Mr. Tigrel's example is a horse by the name of Muhammed. In August 1912 he gave the following problem:

$$(\sqrt{169} + \sqrt{529}) \times (\sqrt{81} - \sqrt{25}) = ?$$

The horse's attention being drawn to a picture of a pheasant left in the stable, he at first wrongly answered 12, but after the picture was taken away, he gave the correct answer, 144. Again, another horse, Czarif, was asked to solve a relatively easy problem, $\sqrt{49} + \sqrt{36} = ?$ His answer was 13. When he was told that this answer was for addition, not multiplication, he still gave the same answer. Realizing that the horse was obstinate, the scientist changed the question to: $\sqrt{49} + \sqrt{36} = ?$ The horse immediately gave the answer 42.

Although I did not feel like talking about such things, I included them simply as examples. There are many other such examples. It has gradually become known that animals are not what we have thought but that some understand human speech quite well.

(Human Beings, p. 90)

Concerning the Australian aborigines mentioned in the above passage from Mr. Ishikawa's book, let me say one thing in their behalf. So long as they are human beings, they cannot be inferior to the chimpanzee. A scholar tested an aborigine whose ability had not been fully developed, and compared him with a fully trained chimpanzee capable of counting beyond ten. This is an error. An aborigine exposed to proper ability development from babyhood should demonstrate fine ability, while a chimpanzee will remain a chimpanzee no matter how he is raised.

However, it is startling news for human beings that the horses Muhammed and Czarif in Professor Tigrel's report could be trained to handle this much math. The effort and research involved in developing the horses' ability can be used as reference. I am sure it was done by the same method as my approach to ability development. I think these examples clarify how awe inspiring the *power created through habit formation* can be.

A small amount of daily training creates astonishing power. In addition to the above examples, this must be found in countless historical cases of the creation of master artists and skilled experts. If human ability can be developed to the extreme, it demonstrates power beyond ordinary people's imagination. I consider the ability that belongs to this realm "demonstration of flawless intuition *(kan)*." When focusing on training the student until intuition develops and on fostering his ability to the extreme, we arrive for the first time at the destination of what I call talent education. I would like to discuss intuition in a later chapter.

While one is giving daily training and helping the child form a habit, it is important, as I said before, to get him interested. In response to the question of how to teach children math, I think something like the following might be done.

First, suppose you are to teach today four additions: $4 + 5 = 9$, $6 + 2 = 8$, $4 + 4 = 8$, $3 + 2 = 5$. Have them practice these five or six times. The next day these additions should be repeated again, but have them practice the set in different orders, with numbers switched around. In other words, let them solve $4 + 5$, $5 + 4$, $6 + 2$, $2 + 6$, $4 + 4$, $3 + 2$, $2 + 3$, and so on. Next, check how many minutes it takes them to do all of these. If a child finishes in ten minutes, then make him promise: "Let's do them in eight minutes tomorrow." The time should be reduced to six minutes the day after; then suggest that he do them in three minutes the following day, helping him gradually speed up.

In the end he will do the additions in one minute. When he has that ability, gradually add more problems: $7 + 3 = 10$, $8 + 2 = 10$, or $6 + 4 = 10$, $5 + 6 = 11$, and so on. Then help him shorten his time again. The crux is to continue to add the kinds of things about which the child feels no pain at all and to train him in shortening the needed time, while advancing him in the level of math. Ability is created where there is repetition, and the proof of that should be measured by the speed of solving problems on the spot.

As the child gradually acquires real ability, he begins to demonstrate the ability to deal with greater quantities of things within shorter periods of time, which allows increased frequency of training. If the child is gradually introduced to more difficult things, he will not think them hard. The above is the instructional method based on the idea that the power of habit creates human ability.

The growth of ability or talent signifies development in undesirable as well as desirable directions. It should be understood that there are no eyes, no heart, no good or evil, no skillfulness or clumsiness to the direction in which ability itself develops; its nature is to develop wherever it is trained and guided frequently. Therefore, the result of ability development is not necessarily a strength that people delight in and praise. Because ability has this nature, instructors who guide students in proper directions are precious; it is up to them whether ability develops toward the good and skillful, or toward the bad and clumsy. If one understands the nature of ability, one understands this.

Suppose proper practice is done five times and wrong practice is done eight times on the same things, the result is as if only wrong practice has been done. This applies to current calligraphy education in schools. It is illogical to fix a session specifically for calligraphy so that children can practice just two hours or so a week and to expect that they can learn to write well with ink and brush. Since practice consists of imitating a well-calligraphed model, naturally we find well-shaped and -arranged characters in calligraphy exhibits. However, this does not represent the children's real ability since these are "imitation" characters made to look like those in their models. The pencil or pen writing in their notebooks demonstrates their true ability. A comparison between their notebooks and ink and brush calligraphies will make this clear.

Even if a child learns the shapes of characters looking at his model, the frequency of calligraphy training is much less than that of daily training in sloppy notebook writing. Therefore the child's ability develops toward the frequently practiced shapes of characters written in his notebooks. Those characters represent his true ability in calligraphy. If this is recognized, in order to carry through the true purpose of calligraphy, one must focus attention first on daily calligraphy practice in small amounts, or on daily training in notebook calligraphy. Marking should be based on notebooks, and model characters must be written in notebooks.

When knowledge of ability changes, the focus of instruction thus changes greatly. If I add a little here in relation to the nature of ability, I always tell my students to practice as follows: "If you make a mistake once while playing, make sure you slowly and correctly play that section more than three times, for making a mistake once means giving yourself wrong training once."

If one thinks this way, one's practice method improves. If the one hour practice is repetition of only what is correct, it is really effective, and the student rapidly improves despite the small amount of practice time. On the other hand, those who, lacking this idea of practice, simply practice vigorously and blindly four or five hours often become worse and worse as they practice, because they are repeating the practice of wrong skills.

These fall into the category of so-called clumsy dilettantes. As far as ability goes, even they have developed ability, but in the direction of clumsiness. It is extremely difficult to correct such people, for it requires returning the debt of clumsiness trained with considerable effort before starting to save for the account called skill. In the case of an adult, an entire lifetime is not enough.

Clumsy dilettantish love of an art is the clearest example to show that effort alone is not the condition for becoming accomplished.

Everyone has ability; yet since it develops where there is training, without regard to good or evil, skillfulness or clumsiness, many different kinds of ability are fostered in society. This shows that there are skillful and clumsy ways of studying. Both instructors and students ought to be clearly aware of this. There is an important knack to skillful or clumsy instruction, and it makes one realize how important it is to help students become efficient learners.

CONCENTRATE ON ONE THING

The purpose of ability development, in brief, is to create a highly active brain. In order to achieve this, I would like to recommend focusing on *a single area* and fostering the bud of ability in that area, whether math, language, art, music, dance, or something technical - it is fine to choose any one of these or any other field.

The expression "He who chases after two hares gains neither" applies to ability development extremely well.

If you wish your child to advance in a scientific field, focus on math. If you wish to develop his ability in art, instruct him in language, music, drawing and painting, or brush calligraphy. Whatever the area, if ability is fostered through training in that single area to a level deemed extraordinary, through that ability the child will later easily comprehend and digest other subjects.

This is what I have experienced. My students whom I begin teaching when they are four or five grow up and enter elementary school, and by the time they are second or third graders they are already playing advanced material known as the world's masterpieces. These include Mozart's Concertos nos. 4 and 5, Corelli's "La Folia," and Bach's "Concerto in A Minor." When the children learn to play these pieces, their faces begin to change: they become more focused, eyes shining with intellect. When I notice this change, I make it a rule to ask the child's parent, "How is he doing at school?" The answer is always this: "He is the best student in his class, thank you." I teach twelve or thirteen such children who are the best at school. The report cards of four or so of them say "Highest Honors." Inferring from this, I came to believe that, when ability is fostered in one area, the child comes to comprehend other things easily as well through the functioning of a well-developed brain. Compare the level of what my students learn at school with the level of music they play in my class. The level of the music is far higher.

Mozart's Concertos nos. 4 and 5 are big pieces which soloists play in concert, and among the pieces used for music school graduation exams in Berlin. In terms of academic education, these pieces are probably the equivalent of college level. If the child has reached this degree of brain function, it is natural that he proves tops in his class at school.

From my experience I would like to recommend this: "Foster your children's ability with concentration from early childhood in one chosen area to an accomplished, high level." Undoubtedly, this is the way to create a brain which works with the highest efficiency. Parents of children whose ability has developed sometimes ask me: "We are not thinking of making our child a musician. What would you suggest we do now?" I always answer:

Neither am I instructing these many children with the intention of turning all of them into musicians. I am doing my best because I would like your child to develop an active brain and a beautiful character. Since his path will open in the future somewhere as a result of family environment, parental ideas, and his own desires, it will be fine for him to continue academic studies as he proceeds to middle school, high school, and college. In brief, the reason that I help create this type of ability in childhood is that I believe the child will demonstrate brilliance no matter what area he enters in the future. There is no reason why your child has to become a musician just because he is studying violin.

My goal in instructing young children is of course to create outstanding musicians spontaneously out of many students, and in fact many who have become musicians are now actively engaged in music-making in concerts and on the radio. However, the other big goal is *to create outstanding people with brains that work.* And it is my hope to nurture a beautiful heart through the power of music. This hope is reflected in my lessons in the form of training. When the child is about six, I start to assign other homework besides violin practice.

To give an example, after the lesson I tell the child without letting the mother hear: "From today on, straighten the shoes or wooden clogs whenever there are guests at home. This is your assignment. Do it so that nobody catches you. Keep it secret from your parents, too, until they find out." At the next lesson, I ask the child in a small voice: "Did you do the homework with the wooden clogs?" The child nods in the affirmative. "Are you not caught yet by your father or mother?" "I'm not caught yet," he answers. "Good; keep at it diligently until you are caught," I say, assigning it again as homework. The child seems happy about doing a good deed in secret. Thus I think up various things, giving just one assignment at a time.

Eventually the mother reports, pleased: "My child has come to behave quite differently. In violin, too, he used to have had enough after five minutes of practice, but it became ten minutes, then fifteen minutes, and now he smoothly practices half an hour, as if he has started to feel he needs to practice." When this happens, it is now safe; the child begins to make rapid progress. His concentration has begun to reinforce itself. "Combining every power," a phrase often used today, signifies the most important thing in the demonstration of a person's ability. If his strength is constantly scattered in all directions, he cannot hope to achieve superior results.

Japanese schools make an egregious mistake on this point. Throughout Japan they put brakes on children's ability until they are seven. What method do they use to develop their ability beautifully when they finally do enter school? They use the clumsiest kind of instruction, that is, the scattering of power, by instructing children in various subjects simultaneously. Moreover, they do not particularly think about the conditions under which ability can be fostered, but unawares lead ability to wither; and they seem blindly to put the curriculum on a conveyer belt.

What will happen when one begins studying two foreign languages at once? What ability will be fostered when one starts studying three languages together? Compare such situations with that of studying only one foreign language. This area needs no further experimentation: everyone knows that the more a person's ability is split, the duller the demonstration of his strength.

In short, what I emphasize is that some measure needs to be taken in school education so that children will be able to concentrate their interest on one thing, whatever it is, and to do their best to develop their ability. I have also observed the children who play the violin beautifully in my class to see if they lose their childlikeness. While playing violin, they concentrate so well that adults wonder how they can demonstrate such ability, but away from their instruments they are perfectly innocent ordinary children, and nothing special is found in them.

The young violinists' concert I hold at Hibiya Public Hall is always well attended by a full-house audience of 3,500 to 3,600. The children seem very happy and excited about this concert, and all perform successfully before the big audience. I stay backstage to send the children out onto the stage by turns according to the program, and listen to their performances with no anxiety because I know, through regular lessons, their real ability to play without the least error.

Adults worry when their turn is coming up and feel uselessly threatened thinking what they would do if they made a mistake; children have no such worries, however, and play even better than usual. It is even necessary for a child-catcher to go around saying, "Haruko, it's getting to be time for you to be ready."

When I hand the child her violin, she briskly walks out on stage with it. Then she plays so calmly and beautifully that one would never know she was running around giggling until just a minute ago. A big piece can take twenty to thirty minutes; but once the child starts to play, she concentrates her entire spirit and performs better than usual with no insecurity. Some among the audience listen with tears.

On returning backstage after the performance, the child puts her violin in her case, and again runs around with the other children. Those who visit them backstage are surprised by the big difference between the on-stage and backstage children.

Children's "growing without childlikeness" has little to do with the superior development of their ability. The cause is found in their character education, that is, how character is formed by the environment; the undesirable phenomena which concern people, I am convinced, are never caused by the development of ability. I say this from my observations not only of concert days but also of the children's daily lives.

In order to let ability be fully demonstrated it is crucial to have the instructional goal of creating an individual excellent in one area or one skill. National education policy should also focus on this point. It is an urgent matter to make a bold decision now to carry out educational innovation with the above idea so as to develop human ability to a high degree, not only within the scope of elementary schooling but at every level of education.

THERE IS NO HARM IN EARLY EDUCATION

It is said that too much intellectual development from early childhood on results in physical infirmity or is an impediment to brain development. However, my experience suggests that this is mere conjecture.

Many of the young children I have taught have developed ability that led people to think them geniuses; however, no such negative effects as people fear have ever been observed. Neither is there any evidence that early education has made the children physically fragile.

What scholars maintain cannot all be considered valid. In academic circles what is deemed correct today, sometimes proves to be the precise opposite of past theories, and what is published today must be completely changed tomorrow. It is no good swallowing scholars' theories unexamined: the true cause of the damage of early education should be found elsewhere than in early education itself.

When I say there is no injury in early education, in addition to my own experience I offer the following reason. If developing children's intellect too early brings about some injury, language learning should present a problem. No other training is as exciting and stimulating as learning language, which a child learns through ceaseless daily training from infancy. Moreover, the people around him force the child to make progress rather rapidly by speaking to him in a language he does not understand. As every child is subject to daily early education, every child's intellect should be totally exhausted.

However, despite early education in language and ensuing ability development, no abnormality results in the child's brain; I have never heard that children who have mastered speech suffer brain damage or become physically fragile as a result. If scholars admit as part of their scholarly theory that making the child's brain work through teaching speech injures it, I will modify my theories, however, unless that is so, I believe there is nothing to worry about in early education.

When one observes how a baby gradually learns to speak, one realizes that the process always follows the steps of imitation, recognition, and development of ability. If cramming occurs, the baby pays no attention to what he does not understand. It is nature's greatness that no forcing works, and there is no cramming at all that forces the brain to work beyond its capacity. If the method of ability development is as natural as in the training of speech, I think no injury can occur there.

It is different if you adopt a forced, wrong method by making a child sit at the desk all day in the manner of entrance exam study or by clumsily forcing on him what he dislikes. You need not worry at all that a child suffers damage from skillfully administered early education.

Some worry that "children may lose their childlikeness." Like the cause of injury to the brain and health, the cause of lost childhood, too, should be found elsewhere than talent education or early education. It is necessary to examine carefully the presence of other causes which inevitably lead to such results.

ACTIVE BRAIN, ACTIVE HEART

As I said above, besides violin homework, I assign young children various chores such as putting guests' shoes neatly together and polishing their fathers' shoes. I would like to describe a little further my reason for doing this.

I believe this serves as preparatory training for further brain function and stimulates the budding of the active heart. Although this belongs to the area of character education rather than talent education, young children's talent education must always be accompanied by character education which fosters their heart. The power of music to develop a human heart is indeed great; yet unless this is reinforced by action in daily life, it does not come alive.

At music school four or five students come to my room together for their lessons. Each observes the others' lessons as well as takes his own lesson. One cold winter morning, I purposely left the window in a corner of the room partly open. Soon four or five students came in. As I watched feeling curious as to what they would do, one of them rose at once, walked to the windows, and closed the one that was open. As a violin student he was far better than the others. What did this mean? I said to the students:

> The one who stood up and closed the window was Yamamoto. I knew that he would do so. To tell you the truth I had kept it open a little as an experiment. I wanted to show you whose brain, of the five students here, was most active, whose heart made its owner close the window. I would like you to think *what poor work the heart of those wrapped up in themselves can demonstrate.*

> There are around us innumerable things to do for others and for society. To create an active mind which works for others and an active heart which serves others with sincerity is the best and fastest way to improve in violin. You agree that Yamamoto is the best player of the five. The experiment just now has proved that his heart is the most active. Those selfish people who only think of themselves make no progress in violin; there is no beauty of performance, no depth. The reason is that the mind does not work. I would like you to think well about the principle of bowing, or what part of the bow should have power, which I always talk about.

Let me briefly explain what I mean by the principle of bowing or the bow's power. I have a motto hanging on the wall in my classroom both for my students and myself: "Do not play; let the bow play."

I have been studying the principle of violin bowing for fifteen or sixteen years, and these words are the conclusion born of it. They can be called the core of my principle of bowing at present. I have thought much about the principle of bowing, and through it actually trained myself, if not yet satisfactorily. I am sure I need to proceed more deeply with my study throughout my life; however, this is the point I have reached at the end of these years.

"Do not play" means that, whether trying to produce beautiful tone or overcome technical difficulty, you fail to achieve it as long as your own power - namely, the ego - works, and as long as you retain your self-centered mind, thinking that you will produce fine tone. That heart obstructs the mindless bow, and the bowing becomes all the more unnatural, and the technique, the heavier, losing the beauty of tone. If a beginner produces an unpleasant, crunching noise, the bow is not the culprit; the noise is produced from the ego-centric force when the student mistakenly thinks that power, that is, he himself, is to play the violin. On the other hand, if you shift your own power to the bow and succeed in making the bow a thing with a beautiful life, the bow produces beautiful tone and works freely. In other words, the less ego there is, the more full of life is the bow. Hence, what we need to study should be how to hold the bow, and how to give it life. As a result of this quest, I have come to teach this as a method: "Hold the tip of the bow." In other words, discard the power with which you hold the bow, and think of concentrating your power at the tip of the bow; achieve equally balanced power in every part of the bow, and make the bow so sharp that it cuts if you touch it. After you have trained in this bow hold, free yourself from egoistic force so it will not obstruct the bow, and let the bow have its own life. This is my creed: "Don't think you are the one to play; let the bow do the playing." It is not just a matter of violin playing; this has been the first creed of my life. In order to create a beautiful world, or at least to make our living environment a beautiful paradise of the heart, we need to shake off our greed. When I use my heart with the utmost sincerity and only for the joy and happiness of others, a beautiful tone, a beautiful heart, and a world of sincerity will surely be created as by the violin bow, and I believe others and I will all be able to live pleasantly.

In the olden days, a swordsman by the name of Kintaro Uno poked a paper lantern with *koyori,* rice paper twisted tight into a string. The paper string easily pierced the oiled paper without causing the flame inside to move. A sword, by contrast, would stir a wind and make the flame flicker as it slit the lamp shade of rice paper. The episode shows how a small piece of paper can accomplish something with no resistance and commotion. This is a very interesting example demonstrating, through a paper string, where power works. When we write with a brush, too, it is only when we discard our own power and let the brush live, that beautiful calligraphy can be produced. Likewise when a master craftsman uses a plane or chisel: when a proper amount of power gathers at the tip of the blade, the result is sharp.

In arriving at the realm of mastery in any skill, one experiences the location of power gradually shift from the self, a self-centered attitude is cast away, and utmost sincerity becomes directed toward the object outside of the self. Then for the first time is one able to enter the realm of the master. In whatever field, the cause of clumsiness is persistence in egoistic greed, egoistic power. Therefore, I make the above principle of bowing the creed of my life. I believe in the heart that discards the self and extends sincerity to others; to put this heart into practice, nurture it, and let it work is the Way. I dream that if all Japanese live making this heart their heart, an ideal world will cultivate itself. Having come to know this Way through music, I am living in order to approach it.

As our past history indicates, the Way is what Japanese people constantly seek. Tea is normally just tasted and drunk, but there is heart in ceremonial tea drinking, and there the Way is sought and becomes *sadoh,* the Way of Tea. In Japan, the sword or bow and arrow, too, becomes the way of self-discipline and sincerity as the Way of the Sword or the Way of the Bow. There is the Way in painting or in flower arrangement. Whatever the field, the ultimate purpose is in training the self, seeking sincerity, and finally dedicating the self to the Way. Regardless of what the subject is, here for the first time a beautiful world will be born.

I have entered too deeply into the principle of violin playing. To sum up, I discovered my creed through my quest for the principle of violin playing, and, viewing this as the Way of Music, I am wishing that it will be put to use in Japanese life. For this reason I am attempting to adopt this in various forms in character education for young children.

MEMORY AND ABSORPTION

Memory can also be fostered and developed as ability. Many of the music school students I teach have a hard time memorizing for performance. That is because they study with the printed music in front of them; those with that habit feel insecure without the music.

Students sometimes ask me: "What can I do to memorize?" They ask this question because what they do so helplessly is to memorize the music with their eyes and try to play from that visual memory.

"Do you feel insecure or visualize the music with your eyes when you sing the national anthem, *Kimigayo?*" "I can sing *Kimigayo* even if I am thinking of something else," the student answers. "Then why don't you practice in such a way that your piece becomes like *Kimigayo?*" I answer. The problem arises from the habit of practicing while looking at the printed music; if one continues practicing every day without the music, one forms the habit of playing by heart so that eventually one can play it, just as one can sing *Kimigayo,* while thinking of something else.

In the case of small children, since I teach them so that there will be no such worry, none has the kind of insecurity that music school students harbor.

In instructing small children, I teach no musical notation at first; I always teach them without the written music. Since the selection of pieces to be taught and the order in which they are taught have much to do with the student's progress, I give a copy of my own selection of violin pieces to the child's mother, and proceed with the instruction in that order.

As noted above, in my lesson it is a rule that the student always plays without the written music, and I instruct only in the material that the student can play in front of me without the music. Because I use this approach also in music school, students who practiced with their eyes glued to the music prior to admission to the school feel greatly troubled. However, it is a matter of habit; they learn to play without insecurity when made to form the habit of playing by heart.

Written music was originally something that was recorded for the sake of reference; it is quite wrong to form a habit so that one cannot play without looking at it. While it is wonderful that a convenient thing called musical notation was invented, when misapplied, it leads to overdependence on the written notes and creates problems as described above. It is good to let written music serve its original purpose; harm that is done by misusing it is the responsibility of the person harmed by it.

Young children under my care form the habit of learning without the music, and as they learn a few dozen pieces, their speed of learning a piece, that is, their memory, improves greatly. So that they can understand the written music by the time they are six or seven, I begin teaching them musical notation little by little approximately six months ahead of time. Therefore they do have the ability to look at the music for the sake of reference when they practice at home. However, they are encouraged to form the habit of practicing without the music once they have used it a little at home. At each lesson, the child hands the book to me, and while listening to him play, I write in remarks where he needs to correct himself. Then I pick out a particularly difficult passage from these places and have him practice until he can play it five times without failure. Even if he can play four times correctly, if he makes even a small mistake the fifth time around, this passage is carried over as homework until the next lesson. This is so that he will be able to play the hardest part best.

When children are trained in this way, their ability changes so much that it is amusing to watch. For example, if a guest enters the room while they are playing a fairly difficult piece, their eyes will follow him, and even their heads will move in his direction. They will be unconsciously drawn to the guest. Will they make mistakes? No, they will continue playing calmly without particularly stumbling. "Where are you facing?" I ask, and, surprised, they will resume their good posture and continue to play eagerly. In such a case, I smile thinking of how interesting children are. Children trained this way innocently and smoothly play without ado the pieces adults perspire to play.

It is evident that children's memory and absorption gradually increase through this way of training. The best examples are two of my disciples, Koji Toyota and Kenji Kobayashi. Suppose I decide that they freshly start learning Mozart's Concerto no. 4 or 5 today and assign it before they go home for the next lesson a week from today, when they will play the entire first movement for me. The movement takes twelve or thirteen minutes to play, and is at least four pages long. In my experience, a music school student, even a superior one, takes at least a month before he can play a comparable piece in front of the teacher without a mistake. I remember spending a month myself when I studied with Professor Klingler in Berlin. However, a child's memory and ability advance by the above instruction to the extent that they can learn the movement in a week.

It is a fact that *those trained from early childhood in memory and absorption demonstrate a totally different level of ability.* This is beyond ordinary imagination, and we must realize how important it is that a child's ability is fostered properly and well. Isn't it a grave matter that this ability grows step-by-step more powerful without knowing where to stop?

To repeat, perhaps I can paraphrase the talent education method as "the method of developing the child's ability while observing his actual strength and giving proper training toward that actual strength." It is, moreover, the simplest method. However, by this method of instruction, progress is extremely slow in the beginning. This resembles having to blow vigorously when making a charcoal fire in a hibachi and there is only a little starter fire. When you rest even a little, the fire threatens to go out. It takes much work, but it is necessary to keep blowing. When other pieces of charcoal gradually catch on, turning a little red, it becomes somewhat easier, and you don't have to blow as hard as at first; the fire now starts even if you blow on and off. When you patiently blow on a while longer, the force of the fire greatly increases. At this point the fire has enough heat and energy so that you no longer have to blow.

The task of the mother and the instructor corresponds to adding the live charcoal and blowing, that is, starting the fire. The way the fire called ability started in the many children I have fostered closely resembles the charcoal catching fire. At first it is as slow as I have described; much time and energy are required when ability is in the kindling stage. But once the fire starts, the speed of the increasing force of fire is extremely fast. Ability develops with accelerated speed, and gains surprising strength. For the first time then, the effect of talent education becomes evident. A little disciple who is a hard worker started to play Bach's Chaconne, one of the hardest pieces, in the third year of her study. This was never expected in the first year: the child was really slow at the start, as I kept her from advancing in the effort to let her gain precision, and instructed her while letting her mark time. If talent education is practiced correctly, every child should make progress similar to everybody else's; but if real effort is made, ability is doubled, as fire burns with vigor where there is effort.

After children reach a certain level, the force of the fire of children who study a normal amount and those who make particularly great efforts, their fire spreading in all directions, begins to differentiate them. Even in three years a great gap emerges. This is the reason that character education which encourages effort is needed in addition to talent education. Let me show the comparative progress of the two groups of children in the following chart:

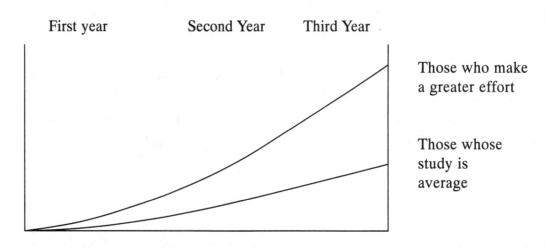

No significant difference appears in the first year. In the second and third years, the difference becomes clear.

Moreover, diligent children who make a special effort every day can correct themselves faster than those who do a normal amount of study. Through their effort, therefore, they form good habits of longer hours of training, and the ability and actual strength acquired through this effort create more strength. Every child practices barely five minutes daily at the beginning, but a child whose mother helps create diligent character and habits begins to practice twenty minutes when others learn to practice ten minutes, one hour when others begin practicing twenty minutes. Since practice time is accumulated every day, it is obvious that a great gap is created in one or two years.

If the strength that increases at such a rate and with such great force continues to be developed, it is natural that extraordinary ability will be demonstrated. If children become diligent and able to make efforts, they will demonstrate remarkable ability. The educational system of our country fails in that it leaves the bud of ability in a state of enervation or virtual death; starts schooling all at once at age six; has children take the same pace each year; and applies brakes so that they do not go beyond a certain limit even if there are children who make a special effort and have more ability than required, so that no child, however outstanding, can advance to materials above graduation from elementary school.

If brakes are put on every child's ability in Japan as perfectly as this, there is absolutely no hope for Japanese people to develop and enhance themselves in the future. I can prophesy this with confidence.

FOSTER INTUITION

Among my young students is a blind boy by the name of Teiichi Tanaka. He was five when his father brought him to me. The father said, "When this child was a baby, the doctor said he would not live unless he had an operation on both eyes. Although we pitied him, we finally went through with the operation, thinking that eyes weren't as important as life; so he lost his sight as a baby and both his eyes are false. As a parent I wished to bring the joy of at least one candle to this boy's dark and unfortunate life, and so, I thought, being able to perform and understand music might give him the greatest happiness. This is why I have come to ask you to teach him violin."

Looking at the lovely blind boy standing there leaning on his father's knees, I wished to somehow give this unfortunate child the joy of playing the violin and knowing the world of music. However, since I had no experience in teaching a blind child, I did not feel confident enough to agree naively to take him. Nevertheless, sympathizing with the father who wished for the child's happiness, I wished somehow to find a way to teach him to play.

"Right now I have neither a method nor experience, so please let me think about it for one week," I answered, and we parted promising to meet again after a week. After finishing my students' lessons that evening, I withdrew into my study and started to think seriously about my new assignment.

First, I shut the light in my study and sat in the dark. Imagining myself blind, I thought about what could guide a blind man to whom the world is pitch dark with no distinction between up and down. He cannot see the shape of the violin that is put in the hand, yet he has to move the bow straight and across a single string without so much as touching the other strings. If the bow position is even half a centimeter off, the bow will rub the next string. How was I going to be able to teach a blind child to do such a delicate thing with ease? Starting with this question, I tried to study this way and that, placing myself in the position of a five-year-old blind child who holds something called a violin and is handed another thing called a bow.

After a while I rose and, taking my violin in my hand, started to play in the dark. Of course I could play with no difference whether in a light place or in this dark room. Then why was I able to feel the same in the dark as in a light place? Even in total darkness I knew how my bow moved and where its tip was; I could feel the locations of the four strings perfectly. Why was this?

While I played thinking of these things, my mind reached a clear solution: "If I help the blind boy see the bow and violin as I can see them when playing in the dark, he will surely be able to learn to play as well as children who can see." In other words, I realized that he would be able to do it if I could give him the mind's eye.

Here finally I felt confident about teaching the blind boy. After a week, Mr. Tanaka came with his son as he had promised. So I told him what I thought, and, asking him to cooperate with me in helping the child study according to my instruction, I decided to begin.

First, I wished to give him the most important training, which would help the boy see the bow. "The violin bow is this kind of thing," I said, placing the bow in his right hand and having him feel the bow to the tip with his left. Then, I said, "Move your right hand, which is holding the bow, up and down." Teiichi moved his bow hand diagonally up and down. "Up and down goes this way," I said, taking his hand and teaching him the vertical motion. When I said, "This time move it left and right," the bow moved again diagonally up and down. "Right and left is this way," I said, again taking his hand in order to teach him the horizontal motion.

"Practice this at home every day, all right?" I explained well, then went on: "Now, let's try an interesting game. First hold out your left hand; then practice poking your left with the tip of the bow, which is in your right hand, five times in a row. Now, try it." This was the project to which I attached the greatest importance. When he tried, the tip of his bow wandered in unexpected directions. It was even dangerous, the bow threatening to poke his ear. Because intuition had not developed, he had no idea where the tip of his bow was.

"Try holding the tip of your bow with your left hand. Right, right. That's where the tip is. All you need to do is to poke your left hand with that tip." The boy tried to do as told, but it was not easy for him to poke his left hand with the tip of the bow.

"This is all for today. Practice it every day until the next time you come, and see how many times out of five you can poke. I will be looking forward to the next lesson, so work hard at it," I said, concluding the first lesson. For a little child, even something like this means a new world: he seemed very happy as he left.

At the next lesson Mr. Tanaka said, "I had Teiichi try, but it is so hard that he couldn't do it well." So I had the boy try just to see: he could move the bow up and down more or less perfectly, but could poke the left hand with the bow only two or three times in five tries. However, even this was great progress, and I thought that a tremendous amount of effort must have gone into it.

"You have improved a lot. Let's continue practicing the up-and-down and left-and-right movements, and the exercise in poking the left hand with the tip of the bow until you can do it five times in a row correctly. Today I am adding another new thing, so please practice this one, too," I said, adding a new exercise. This was to grab with the left hand the tip of the bow held in his right hand in one try, without groping in the air but moving his hand directly to where he believed the tip was. It was an exercise in sensing where the tip of the bow was.

This, too, was difficult to accomplish on the first day, and I finished the lesson leaving it at that. However, through daily training, in two weeks or so Teiichi was able to poke his left hand with the bow with precision five times in a row, and also grasp the tip of the bow. So then I gave him a new assignment: "Let's practice poking the left thumb with the tip of the bow. Learn to do it five times in a row." The object to be poked at changed suddenly in size from the palm to the thumb. Mr. Tanaka, who seemed to have struggled hard with this assignment, commented at the next lesson: "The practice this time was very difficult; it was really hard work." But when I had Teiichi try, he could hit at least once in five times.

"Now, let's see how your teacher will do," I said, and picking up my bow, tried to poke my left thumb. I was caught by surprise, finding it quite challenging. Even for one who can see, it is hard to poke something by a movement parallel to oneself, although it is possible to poke a point which one faces - the bow being a long object, it creates an unexpected optical illusion which makes aiming all the more difficult. Then, this was too difficult for Teiichi. In the order of things, I should have assigned something a little easier, such as poking a matchbox held in the left hand. Despite this impossible instruction, however, thanks to Mr. Tanaka's effort - training has a fearsome power - eventually Teiichi was able to hit his thumb two or three times out of five.

Since the tip of the bow was thus clearly visible to the mind's eye of the boy, and the directions of up-and-down and left-and-right motions also became precise, I believed that it was now fine to start violin practice and at last began lessons. Naturally, they were not successful at first while he was still unused to the violin, but, as a result of the bow training described above, he soon began to play well like other children. In about a year, having learned to play skillfully Beethoven's Minuet, Boccherini's Minuet, and elementary concertos, he became one of the fine performers at my young students' concert at the Hibiya Public Hall. When this blind boy played at the Hall, many women listened with tears.

In the above account of starting violin instruction for a blind child, the central idea is the development of *kan,* or intuition. In order to advance to the point where intuition develops normally, usually the first step is to achieve security through the use of the eyes, a faculty for measuring the object; then this is followed by thorough training. Then intuition starts to develop. When intuition has developed, one can then do the same thing with eyes closed. In this case, intuition is not in the motion of the eyes but in the activity of the brain. Moreover, this brain power is not at the level of *thinking* about something, but is a far higher, instantaneous ability to *accurately anticipate something and act accordingly.* This is the highest and greatest ability that a human being can possess. Intuition is not slow-moving, tepid brain activity, but the ability to instantly anticipate the *proper consequence* which should appear as a result of the action, or the ability to sum up all the possibilities and unerringly find the answer. I can compare these two different kinds of ability in my own playing.

For example, when playing the perfect center of the E string, the thinnest of the four violin strings, one can achieve speed like a flash in a fast passage, ringing that single point and moving to the next tone in several tenths of a second. However, this can happen as many times as desired with no error at all: by the power of intuition created through practice, one can do this with no problem. However, when one *thinks* as one plays, which is below intuitive power, it does not work. In other words, intuition is lost and intonation always goes off when *the willpower to think* works: I have to measure the right position to play; I'm safe around here; I don't want to make a mistake in front of people, or other similar thoughts.

This is because the thought to play well or the thought to make no mistakes obstructs intuition, causing one to play clumsily or make mistakes contrary to one's expectation. "Thoughtlessness" is an expression of the world of intuition. "Thoughtlessness" in a person without intuition, however, makes him as incapable as an infant. The true intention of those who respect the realm of thoughtlessness should be found here; they do not mean the thoughtlessness of those without intuition.

In an episode everybody knows from long ago, Nasu no Yoichi, amid a large force of friends and foes, shot down a fan hoisted on an enemy boat.[4] This is an example of intuition working beautifully.

I think that everyone called a superb or a master archer throughout history probably had the skill to shoot the target on a fan hoisted on a rolling boat, but Nasu no Yoichi's greatness stems not only from this superior skill. He had a weighty responsibility, shouldering himself the honor of the entire Genji force: should he fail, even if he killed himself by way of begging forgiveness, how, he wondered, was he to save the Genji clan from disgrace? The single arrow he was going to shoot had this grave

---

[4.] On February 18, 1185, when the warring Genji and Heike clans were divided between the sea and the shore, the Genji leader Yoshitsune ordered Yoichi to hit the golden sun on a scarlet fan which a Heike lady hoisted on her small boat, a gesture which the Genjis took to be an invitation to shoot. The youth from Nasu province went a few steps into the water, prayed, took aim, and hit the target. The north wind at dusk happened to subside just then. The fan floated on the white waves, as the Heike and Genji people joined in praise. The episode is recounted in the early thirteenth century *Heike Monogatari* (Tales of Heike).

meaning. His greatness lay in his pulling himself back to "thoughtlessness" like water so that he was able to shoot an arrow with intuition as usual.

If his heart had not been disciplined to that extent, he would definitely have shot an arrow in desperation, thinking uneasily, "No matter what, this arrow must pierce the target." When such a thought was active, his intuition would have been dulled, and his arrow would have missed the target despite his desperate prayer. Again, in prayers for the protection of the gods and the Buddha, if a thought had been there of dependence upon their protection, I think it would have been the same. He could demonstrate on this occasion his constantly trained skill of a hundred hits out of a hundred shots because the action of fine intuition habitually supported his skill and he knew that this was precisely his ability. The way of the arrow by which this power worked was indeed the way of truth which the gods protected, and Nasu no Yoichi never doubted that this way alone led to the target. This is where I find his greatness.

Even if we pray to God, it is impossible to borrow his power without striving to improve our own intuitive power. What is God's power if not to help us achieve this power? This is how I think of intuition.

Watching children play catch, there too I find training in intuition. A's ball flies with precision into B's hand at a fair distance. Suppose the distance is measured, the ball is weighed, the wind's resistance, direction, and speed are calculated, and the ball is sent to the other person's hand by a certain contraption. This may not be impossible with today's science, but if the weight and size of the ball were to change constantly, even today's science would be unable to respond to those changes freely, and in terms of time consumed would be far inferior to human intuition.

Children play catch by the work of intuition which, through hundreds and thousands of instances of training, instantaneously computes the wind's strength, the distance, the ball's weight, and so forth. In every game that lets them demonstrate such ability, children should be trained successfully until they reach beyond a certain level of ability, that is, until intuitive power is created through practice. It is extremely important for them to accumulate brain power this way.

Whether in catch, tennis, or anything else, if we give enough training to children for them to be chosen as players, I believe that it will nurture a strength that will prove helpful in the child's lifework. Even if we look at something like violin playing simply from the technical side, it is full of elements that prompt the demonstration of intuitive power. As I stated earlier, when they advance in violin, children's faces and eyes begin to shine beautifully and have more focus, indicating a change. Everyone agrees that those described as retarded reveal at a glance a lack of focus somewhere in their faces. When the brain starts to work, and moreover work in an advanced way, it cannot be denied that even an adult's face reflects this change.

For this reason a child's education is inadequate unless it is carried to the point where the child's facial expression changes. Changes in the face and eyes do not mean changes in the framework of the face given by the parents; whether one is good looking or not cannot perhaps be controlled. However, some physiological changes certainly can occur, and what might be called the beauty of intelligence emerges spontaneously.

The question of intuition's work is wide in scope, reaching every aspect of human life. Although the examples I have given above were limited to cases where intuitive power works in technical areas, everyone knows that similar power is demonstrated in spiritual matters.

Long ago in the castle town of Nagoya, Miyamoto Musashi (1584-1645), a swordsman, painter, and author of *A Book of Five Rings,* glimpsed a fine samurai coming his way and abruptly said: "You are Yagyu Hyogo, aren't you?" Yagyu Hyogonosuke Toshiyoshi was known to be a sword instructor in the service of Tokugawa Yoshinao of Owari Province.

The samurai thus addressed replied, the story goes, "Yes, I am. You are Master Miyamoto, aren't you?" It is impressive that the two individuals demonstrated this much cognitive power, having never seen each other and being on a journey under a distant sky. It is due to the work of great intuition that, perceiving something radiating from each other's appearance, they instantly judged as they did.

This type of perception, also called "direct sense," is the power to combine and compute every condition in an instant. An outstanding businessman, constantly aware of tomorrow's changes, demonstrates the power to take unerring measures ahead of time. I could probably give endless examples along this line. In brief, a person's ability can without fail reach that level as a result of ability development, and producing people with this power ought to be the ultimate goal of talent education.

We must carefully consider what poor and weak work can be demonstrated by knowledge which consists of mere "knowing." Occasionally, having studied means one's never having used intuition until age twenty-four or twenty-five and having become, through continual cramming, a useless person with erudition and academic records but without a brain that works. There are many examples of such people.

On the other hand, it makes us think to see vast numbers of those who, having actually nurtured great power, play active roles in society as useful individuals with active brains. Here, too, a piece of truth exists; they have not accomplished great things by chance.

From the viewpoint of ability, no matter how many books one reads, no matter what difficult logic is learned, if that represents the so-called cramming which amounts to nothing more than merely walking through the material just once, and if no effort is made to foster the ability to utilize knowledge, then the result is merely an incompetent man of erudition.

Regrettably, many people in our present society have been educated to fit this type. This is because in the past Japan's educational circles have greatly erred in their focus. Japanese people have applied their vigor almost exhaustively to reading the world's books, making the mightiest effort to know everything in the world and imitate everything in the world. This trend has been striking from the Meiji era until today.

For the past several decades, this has been the path Japanese people have walked: their most powerful effort has gone into studying and catching up with every foreign achievement. Despite the fact that this period has lasted as long as several decades, Japan has always followed the world's culture, never even once developing enough to lead the world. This is because our educational principle has been flawed, and we never reached the point where we could demonstrate the true ability which should have been fostered in us.

This one thing should suffice to make us realize the need to reflect deeply on our past and discard the educational principle or method which we have employed over many years. We must adopt a method which will enable us to demonstrate our real ability in international society.

From long ago great men have always been those who had fine intuition. If we rebuild our educational principles so that we produce intuitive people, it will not be impossible for Japan to play a leading role in world culture.

Intuition is not something that is created only in extremely difficult advanced skills; it is an ability spontaneously prepared even in ordinary matters where concentrated training is accumulated. If we focus our educational goal on the single point of training individuals whose intuition works, and continually foster human ability in every area, Japanese people will easily exceed past levels of ability and gradually be able to demonstrate their real strength.

With this idea, when parents heighten their educational principles to the problem of intuition while our national educational principles also focus on the same, I think our future will be brilliant. It is simply a question of discarding the idea of *teaching and advancing* and instead creating Japanese people's ability through *teaching, pausing, and thoroughly training.*

IN SEARCH OF A NEW EDUCATIONAL SYSTEM

As stated above, the elementary school systems enforced since the Meiji era, both the *shogakko* system before the war and the current *kokumin gakko* system, have totally inhibited us from enhancing our ability because they have been intended for homogeneous mass production which does not allow schools to be unique. Then, how should we reform our educational system? We must seek and cultivate the best way with extreme care.

I am sure there are a variety of approaches to educational innovation, but no matter what forms it takes, and what systems institutionalize it, the best remains "the path which does not violate the law of nature and which follows the reason of heaven." This is an immutable principle, and no method that violates this should be taken. The *kokumin gakko* system was created in the name of a great innovation from the old *shogakko* system; however, when the new system was made public, it was seen to be quite similar to the old containing no particular innovation.

The need for reforming the Japanese educational system is serious. The kind of changes involved in turning the *shogakko* into *kokumin gakko* make no sense; we need more fundamental reforms. We must discard the unsuccessful systems and instructional methods of the past, and found a unique educational system on the ambitious new principle of "fostering big trees to create a beautiful forest under heaven."

To do this, the nation has to concentrate its effort on education during the so-called seedling age before school, which has not received much attention in the past. The question of early education, in other words, must be taken up as crucial educational policy.

Home Education

Early education for young children is essential for a high level of national development, and as long as mothers are their first instructors, home education must be greatly emphasized.

Instruction at home always succeeds or fails depending upon the parental attitude, and the effort of the loving mother becomes a powerful educational force superior to all else. However, it is necessary that the method of instruction be well understood. If there is satisfactory understanding, and if the mother is a good instructor and the father a good assistant, the child will always successfully demonstrate his ability.

At present there are families which teach a little math and the alphabet to preschool children, but this is simply intended as preparation for entering elementary school. If it is just this much, it may even be harmful in that the child can do well on entrance: despite the fact that no ability has developed, he does not try to learn because he is relaxed about being able to do well, and often the result is that, contrary to expectation, he falls behind the class before he realizes it. It is perhaps for this reason that officials of the Ministry of Education advocate on the radio that there is no need for preschool preparation. If, however, through early education, - say, in math - the child's ability is truly developed to the fifth- or sixth-grade level by school age, his ability will help him comprehend and digest language and other subjects as well with no difficulty whatsoever.

If the child is allowed to keep on advancing in big strides at home after entering school, there will be no problems. The point is in training the child until he acquires ability. If this is missed and the child is simply taught enough to be prepared for entering school, no ability will develop; it may instead create disaster.

As long as the elementary school system remains the way it is with no better paths to be cultivated, the only alternative will be to adopt the above method of home education to create children's ability. However, if the time comes when special schools are founded which accept capable children by the examination system described below and educate them to high, specialized levels, many educated parents will make enthusiastic efforts to help their children enter such schools by developing fine ability in them. Only if such schools are founded, needless to say, will great parental efforts be made throughout the country toward developing children's ability. In that case I think a vast movement for national enhancement will proceed even if we just stand by. The government authorities should explain this well to the people, and encourage it as a policy.

Kindergarten and Early Education

The present kindergarten[5] gathers young children in a school-like environment of group life with a seeming goal of education in character and intellect preparatory to elementary school. However, viewing its consequences, I find it to be rather ineffective, as if it were nothing more than a kind of child-care center. Even when the leader who runs the kindergarten is both progressive and great as a teacher, he is to do nothing as long as children have to start over again from the alphabet at elementary school. Therefore, kindergarten teachers are naturally limited to the lowly position of giving instruction in relation to elementary school, and being unable to try innovative instruction.

Now such kindergartens will no longer be needed. If every kindergarten can with one leap transform itself into an institution which gives talent education as well as character education for young children, this will give our nation a powerful start. This transformation should be realized by all means; otherwise, great educational betterment will not easily begin.

---

[5] Japanese kindergarten at present is for three-to-five-year-olds, formal schooling starting at age six. In 1946, when the system was not yet widespread, children attended kindergarten for one, or at most, two years.

At the present moment at a converted airplane factory, I am producing various musical instruments for export. When circumstances permit, I would like to found a kindergarten myself and start this movement. Let me call it "special kindergarten." I would like to continue to teach violin there. Since violin can be taught from age three or so, there is no need for a minimum age requirement for entrance into the kindergarten. I know from my past experience that by age seven children can be taught to play the Bach Concerto in A Minor or a Mozart concerto, a level which can perhaps be compared to that of second year students at Tokyo Music School in recent days. In three or four years, children advance to that level.

Again, at this special kindergarten, besides music, I will ask outstanding men of like minds in every area, including math, language, painting, handicraft, and sculpture, to study instructional approaches so that we can successfully foster children in each area, aiming to have today's children demonstrate the level of ability displayed long ago by Arai Hakuseki. *On the basis of what I have been doing for over a dozen years, I know that this is definitely possible; it is no desktop chatter.*

The ability development system for young children must of course eagerly welcome individual instruction not provided for in the framework of school. It is certainly good to give character and talent education to children with a method like the *terakoya* system of the old days, private classes providing basic education for commoner children run by a samurai, priest, or physician in the Edo period. If the teacher has outstanding personality and ability, something like that can be a fine educational organ.

When many children successfully develop their ability by age seven through the efforts of outstanding parents and great teachers, advanced schools will be required to continue their education to higher levels. Establishing such schools will be the very center of Japan's educational innovation, and unless this system is developed, the goal of educational reforms will not be reached. In order to create such a system, we must try our best to influence public opinion and at the same time actively evolve a political movement. I would like tentatively to call this a system of special elementary schools.

Special Elementary School

Let me describe some of my hopes concerning this special kind of school, which has the grave significance stated above.

The special elementary school is a state or private school, founded with the aim of a high leap for the nation and with great expectations. We need to make this a powerful educational organ by working out ample and generous educational budgets, and at the same time by carefully choosing teachers. Private schools with this purpose must of course be sanctioned, but only following careful screening. Entrance into special school should always require entrance exams. For the exams every area of culture in which the nation should excel ought to be considered, regardless of the subject or kind.

Concretely speaking, some children will take the exams in math, others in language, and still others will be tested in abacus, violin or piano, painting, sculpture, calligraphy, Noh drama, or dance. Whatever the area of testing specialized ability, a child should be accepted for further development if, at age seven, he is already accomplished and his ability exceptional. Therefore, the exams should not specify the level of acceptance or limit the areas, but admission should be determined by letting an applicant demonstrate the highest ability he can express, spontaneously revealing his thorough training. Therefore, the exams should test children individually. If teachers specializing in the chosen areas divide the task and take turns, exams will be finished in a week or ten days. If so many children apply that it takes ten days, that is great. It is thoughtless to feel bothered by the time the exams consume; if it takes ten or fifteen days, fine. All applicants should be tested once through. Since the exam subject is just one in each case, it is simple.

As for how to instruct the children admitted, it must be by the method of ability development. In each special subject the child must have a teacher with professional knowledge, and his special skills must be individually taught as is done in music school today. In math and language, the first graders should be divided into smaller groups according to their levels, so that each teacher has a small number of children within a feasible scope for teaching. If one teacher has ten or so students, he will be able to instruct them well.

At this rate, a special school attended by three hundred children requires nearly thirty teachers with professional skills. Since this professional instruction should be accompanied by compulsory classes in general subject, teachers are needed for these also. Moreover, since teachers at this school need to be selected from competent people who can be called authorities in diverse areas, their salaries require sufficient budgets. It is quite natural that we give preferential treatment to these teachers who have the crucial role of carrying out this important national objective. If we satisfy ourselves with average teachers and just innovate the system, there will be no fruit. Teachers of this school should be selected from both government employees and ordinary citizens, for a vast number of great individuals exist among citizens. Since, oddly, in many cases in Japan today, titles have nothing to do with the real ability of the person, a pitifully weak faculty will be formed if we pay attention only to titles.

A child's ability is greatly affected by the real strength of the instructor. If the instructor has sufficient strength and if his method is proper, the child can demonstrate amazing ability. Therefore, teachers of the special school must be instructors with superior ability. Scouting outstanding people with the greatest emphasis on this aspect will clarify the significance of the special elementary school system.

As for the attendance period at special school, I feel we cannot yet determine whether to make it an eight-year or seven-year school. If children enter school at age seven already with fairly advanced ability and study by a proper instructional method in the following years, they will be able to develop to an unexpected height in seven years. I know - although perhaps only through my own experience - that once talent starts to be demonstrated, ability is reinforced visibly with a multiplied or accelerated speed. Therefore, the child can finish the basic steps fast and enter a creative world or innovative area. The desirable period of schooling differs by the area of training, and this is why I cannot choose between seven or eight years before actual experimentation. For now, then, we can make it an eight-year system to allow enough time, while permitting students to take graduation exams in their seventh year. The reason that early graduation should be provided is so that we can let students enter a higher school, that is, a college or a professional school (of the same level as college). When this special elementary school system is created, in-between schools like middle schools or high schools will be naturally superfluous; therefore we should abolish them and children should enter college or professional school directly from the special school.

Those who enter special school by math, language, or other academic subjects can later be enrolled in a specialized course in the chosen subject, and naturally it is necessary that teachers specializing in that area teach that course. If a child studying math wants to go into electricity, he can be instructed in the basics of that field here so he is prepared to be sent to a professional school of electricity. If he enrolls in a specialized course around the time he finishes the fourth year, he has three years to study in the special field even if he is to graduate after the seventh year. Furthermore, graduates of special schools should be admitted to professional schools without entrance exams.

Since professional instructors will teach at the special schools, the school budget will be quite large, but realizing that education alone can reconstruct the nation, Japan as its first policy should budget large sums for the people's education in the future as it spent boldly on military budgets in the past.

To sum up, the following conditions are required:
1. Adopt an entrance exam system (age seven).
2. Give specialized education.
3. Select and invite outstanding individuals from every area as teachers.
4. Appropriate sufficient funds for education.

The details ought to be stipulated to suit reality. I think it has been our great misfortune that we lack a special education system for producing outstanding individuals through such schools.

If a coherent school system for special kindergarten, special elementary school, and college is established, it will inspire confidence. Those who graduate from there each year with superior ability will become a great cultural driving force.

Children will graduate from special elementary school at fourteen or fifteen, and from college, if it is three years, at seventeen or eighteen. In musical circles, outstanding people known to the world have often debuted around seventeen or eighteen. This is proof of the fact that human ability can reach that height by then. I deeply believe that the ability to enter into truly creative work is prepared at that age. Common sense today expects age seventeen or eighteen to correspond to the level of graduation from middle school; however, this is present-day Japan's common sense, and not that of future people with highly developed culture.

When I discuss the system by which graduation from college occurs at age eighteen, I may give an odd impression to the general population. However, when one thinks about starting at age four or five and receiving thirteen or fourteen years of instruction with a focus in a single area, ability such as I describe is naturally created. Children whose talent develops with accelerating speed have the ability to easily break through any difficulty, and this factor must be included in one's calculation.

General Elementary School

For many children who cannot enter special elementary school, or who from the start do not aim to enter there, elementary school is naturally necessary. However, it goes without saying that there, too, instructional methods and educational principles should be based on a study of the truth about ability and undergo major innovations.

At general elementary schools, talent education should be adopted as at the special schools, with children concentrating on one or two major subjects so that every child can easily develop his ability within those subjects, abolishing the greengrocer-style educational principle of versatility.

The period of elementary school should be changed to eight years, and in those eight years, children's ability should be helped to develop at least to the level beyond that of present-day middle school graduates. This is not difficult for children with average ability. The point is to focus on developing human ability which can be naturally achieved and to help people reach sufficient height as cultured people with graduation from elementary school. We must raise the educational level to the point that elementary school is sufficient as general education for future Japanese. If children can be fostered to reach this level, there will be no need for middle school, which is like an extra house added on top of a house.

While abolishing middle school, we must establish a large number of specialized schools in every area and of every kind with direct contact with real society, so that useful, realistic education is given along with on-the-job training. The period of study should be between two and three years, determined according to the need, so as to train people who can be useful actually and instantly. For this purpose horizontal contact should be made in every area; specialized research centers should be installed where new and progressive research will be constantly done; the most advanced, newest knowledge flowing out of those places should be made public and taught at various specialized schools; and the system should each year allow graduates with new, advanced knowledge and skills to flow into society in every area.

To look at the situation in real society, it is an immovable fact that in every country people are engaged in specialized work, with a deepening trend toward *one person, one matter, one talent.* If we consider this, educational principle should not be so tepid as to prepare children to understand a little of everything to a commonsense level. The whole nation should adopt a one-subject, one-talent principle, realizing that excelling in one skill creates the ability to be proficient in many.

My idea is that, whether students are in special or general school, school life should end around eighteen, or, in other words, learning days should end at eighteen. Present-day Japanese are spending one-third to one-half of their lives as learning days within the inefficient educational system. We should sweep away this wastefulness, and make schooling shorter and more efficient. A person's real ability cannot be measured by the length of time spent on learning.

When the educational period is shortened so that every child can be trained to demonstrate ability successfully at age eighteen, Japanese people will be able to develop actively as *a nation with active ability and a long active period.*

Great people called geniuses have entered their active period at seventeen or eighteen, and have already made fairly large achievements by age twenty-five or twenty-six, or thirty. We ordinary mortals wonder how they were able to achieve so much in that period, but I now think that if ability is successfully fostered, people can in fact be most active in that period; and precisely because they engaged in those activities then, they can demonstrate their ability as great men in their thirties and forties as a result of the superior power accumulated through those trials.

"Ordinary people are not necessarily ordinary people" - this should be deeply imprinted on our minds at the first stage of our development.

If we can produce ten thousand outstanding people, this already means nurturing the real ability that enables us to become an outstanding nation. The country must at least do its best to create these ten thousand outstanding individuals. This is a crucial enterprise that today's Japan must start before anything else.

If it is realized that every child or every person is capable, and if general innovative education is advanced creating an era when this ability can be demonstrated, our future will be brilliant.